Expository Sermons on the Epistle of James

BOOKS BY DR. CRISWELL . . .

Expository Sermons on Revelation – 5 Vols. in 1
Expository Sermons on the Book of Daniel, 4 Vols. in 1
The Holy Spirit in Today's World
The Baptism, Filling and Gifts of the Holy Spirit
Expository Sermons on Galatians
Ephesians – An Exposition
Expository Sermons on James
Expository Sermons on the Epistles of Peter
Isaiah – An Exposition
Acts: An Exposition, Volumes 1 and 2

Expository Sermons on the Epistle of James

W. A. Criswell

OF THE ZONDERVAN CORPORATION
GRAND RAPIDS, MICHIGAN 49506

EXPOSITORY SERMONS ON THE EPISTLE OF JAMES
Copyright © 1975 by The Zondervan Corporation
Grand Rapids, Michigan

Fifth printing 1980
ISBN 0-310-22820-4

Library of Congress Cataloging in Publication Data

Criswell, W. A.
　Expository sermons on the Epistle of James.

　　1. Bible. N. T. James—Sermons.　　2. Baptists—
Sermons.　　3. Sermons, American.　　I. Title.
BS2785.4.C74　　　　227'.91'06　　　　75-21120

All rights reserved. No part of this publication may be reproduced, stored in a retrieval system, or transmitted in any form or by any means, electronic, mechanical, photocopy, recording or otherwise, without the prior permission of the copyright owner.

Printed in the United States of America

To
PAT ZONDERVAN

a true Gideon soldier who has marched throughout
the earth for Jesus and whose ministry in books
has touched unnumbered souls for the cause of Christ.

CONTENTS

Foreword
1. The Lord's Brother 11
2. Trials of Our Faith 20
3. Seven Tests of Faith 28
4. Real Religion 36
5. Personal Religion 41
6. Paul's Faith and James' Works 47
7. Orthodoxy of the Devil 55
8. The Untamed Tongue 62
9. Our Words 68
10. Getting Things From God 75
11. The Quality 83
12. The Coming of the Lord 89
13. Patience of Job 96
14. Praise and Prosperity 103
15. Divine Healing 108
16. Effectual Praying 116
17. The Winner of Souls 123

FOREWORD

Music, poetry, and oratory are, unlike works of painted art, common in this respect — they are subjected to lapse of time. When the pastor stands in the pulpit delivering from his soul God's message for the hour, he must be ever mindful of the clarity of the spoken word, thereby including much repetition that otherwise would be omitted in a book that is written out. As you read these sermons, it will be most evident that they were presented to a listening audience.

More than I could delineate to you, God richly blessed the study and preparation of these messages on James. It is my hope that this volume, likewise, will be of infinite value to preachers, teachers, and laymen who seek to honor God as they pray over the Bible and share its infallible word with others.

Surely, as God so bountifully blessed me in preparing the sermons, He no less blessed those who heard them when they were delivered in our church. May He now likewise bless the readers who follow them in their written form.

W. A. Criswell
First Baptist Church
Dallas, Texas

Chapter 1

THE LORD'S BROTHER
(James 1:1)

The Book of James is a very Jewish book, in fact, it is the most Jewish book in the New Testament. The name "James" is a Hellenized form of the Hebrew "Jacob." We begin our discussion of this book by noticing that James is described as "a servant of God and of the Lord Jesus Christ." The word "servant" actually means "slave" so we read "James, a slave of God and of the Lord Jesus Christ, to the twelve tribes." There's no such thing in the Bible as the lost ten tribes. That must be a figment of someone's imagination. Where it came from, I cannot find. There's not even a hint to anything like that in the Bible. "James, a slave of God and of the Lord Jesus Christ, to the twelve tribes." They are here today. God knows them. The word that is used to refer to the scattered is "diaspora" — the twelve tribes of the diaspora — the great scattering of the Jewish nation among the Gentiles. So James writes his letter to the twelve tribes — to the great family of God's chosen people which are scattered among the nations of the world.

Which James?

Who is James? You will find in your study an altogether different idea than what many suppose. At the end of the New Testament we have these short epistles called the General Epistles, so we think that the men who wrote them cannot be compared with those who wrote the larger books that are found at the beginning of the New Testament. Actually, we could not be more mistaken. There are three Jameses in the New Testament. The first one is James, the son of

Zebedee, John's brother. Zebedee and his sons and Simon Peter were fishing partners in Capernaum on the Sea of Galilee. James seems to have been the elder of the two brothers because he always is mentioned first. You never read John and James, but always James and John. He also was the first martyr among the apostles. In A.D. 44 he was beheaded by Herod Agrippa I.

In the New Testament there are two Herod Agrippas. In Acts 12 Herod Agrippa I beheaded James, the apostle. In Acts 26 the apostle Paul addresses Herod Agrippa. He says, for example, "Whereupon, O king Agrippa, I was not disobedient unto the heavenly vision" (v. 19). The first Herod Agrippa in Acts 12 is called Herod — he is Herod Agrippa I. The second Herod Agrippa, the son of the first, in Acts 26 is called just Agrippa. But they are Herod Agrippa I and II — father and son. So James, the son of Zebedee, fulfilled the prophecy of the Lord when He said to him that he would drink of the cup that He drank of and would be baptized with the baptism that He was baptized with, referring to James' martyrdom. So James was cut down and martyred so early in the propagation of the Christian faith that we have no record of his life or testimony.

The second James in the New Testament is also an apostle. He is called James the son of Alphaeus. Sometimes he is called the brother of Joses and son of Mary, but we know nothing about him at all. He is one of the apostles and we have no further knowledge concerning him.

The third James, and the man of great stature in the first church and in the propagation of the gospel in the first century, was James, the brother of our Lord. He is by far the greatest personality in the early church and is without peer or comparison. To us that seems unthinkable, because Simon Peter, the apostle John, and certainly the apostle Paul seem to have been great overpowering characters in those early days of the church. But I am persuaded that the great man of stature in that early church was James, the pastor of the church at Jerusalem and the Lord's brother. It is worth knowing him, and listening to what he has to say.

This James, as I have mentioned, is the brother of our Lord. They had the same mother — Jesus and James were born of the womb of Mary. Jesus was born before she married Joseph, and James after Joseph and Mary were married. That may seem contradictory to

The Lord's Brother

tradition, but tradition is tradition. The Bible plainly avows that Joseph knew not Mary until, *until* she had been impregnated by the Holy Spirit and had given birth to the Lord Jesus. So the Virgin Mary gave birth by the Holy Spirit to the Lord Jesus and then she became the wife of Joseph, of which union the four sons and the unnamed daughters were born. James then grew up in the home with the Lord Jesus. I imagine it would be psychologically difficult for a brother to see and to accept the fact that his older brother was the Messiah, the Son of God. So James did not believe in the messianic ministry of his brother Jesus. He refused it. And he lived all the days of the life of our Lord in unbelief. Matthew and Mark and John describe him in the gospel accounts as being an unbeliever along with the rest of his brethren.

After the resurrection of Christ from the dead He appeared personally to James. He singled him out and had a personal conference with him. After the Lord was raised from the dead He won James to the faith. So much so, that when we read in Acts 1 of the 120 who had gathered in that prayer meeting in the upper room, we notice that James had also won his brothers to the faith. Along with the apostles and disciples, and with Mary his mother, you will find James and his brothers in that first prayer meeting. After that he rose to great stature in the church. For example, when the apostle Paul writes in the Book of Galatians about his conversion in A.D. 37 and his three years in Arabia, he says that he went to Jerusalem and conferred with James — this James.

In Acts 12 we read another interesting comment about James. Simon Peter was liberated from prison, and following his release he went to the prayer meeting of the church and knocked on the door. A young girl named Rhoda came to the door, looked and saw that it was Simon Peter. He who had been prayed for came back to the people who were praying. Rhoda ran into the room and told them Peter was alive — he was at the door. And they said it was not so. Herod Agrippa I who had beheaded James, had put Simon Peter in prison to cut off his head also. To some, Herod Agrippa had already killed Peter and Rhoda was just seeing his spirit. Isn't that a strange thing? Pray and pray and have no idea that God is going to answer your prayers at all! The church in Jerusalem did that — the first church. They said, "Girl, you're just beside yourself. You're just seeing things." "No," said

Rhoda. "He's at the door and knocking. I looked out the window and it's Peter — Simon Peter." So the church got off its knees, rushed to the door, and there stood Simon Peter in the flesh. God's angel had delivered him, and what did Simon Peter say? He told the church to tell James — this James. Tell James what God has done.

The Jerusalem Conference

In about A.D. 47, when the apostle Paul had returned from his first missionary journey, there arose a great controversy in the church. Whenever you see division, controversy, or debate in the church — in the household of faith — do not be alarmed. It has been that way from the beginning. This great controversy arose over Gentiles, for Paul, Barnabas, and the Hellenistic Jews preaching to the Gentiles told them that if they would accept the Lord Jesus, they would be saved. But the church at Jerusalem, hearing about it, said not so. A man could not be saved unless he was first circumcised, and he kept the law of Moses and became a full-fledged Jew. Then he could be saved by adding to the works of Judaism, faith in the Lord Jesus Christ. A great debate developed, so the first Jerusalem conference was called. In that conference we have Paul, Barnabas, and the Hellenistic Jews saying that a man could be saved just by trusting in the Lord. No works. You did not have to be baptized, you did not have to take the Lord's Supper, to be circumcised, to observe clean and unclean. You didn't have to keep the Sabbath day, didn't have to obey laws or regulations, or conduct any rites or rituals to be saved. You were saved just by trusting Jesus. That was one side. The other side consisted of Judaizers who said that in order for a man to be saved he not only had to trust Jesus but he had to do this and this and this and this before he could be saved. Because of this difference there was a great confrontation in the church. Who presided over that confrontation in the first Jerusalem conference? James. Who made the final authoritative decision? James. Who wrote the decree for the church? James. Who placed it in the hands of the apostles for the distribution among the Gentile converts? James. He towered over all the other Christians in that first century.

Now in the second chapter of Galatians Paul describes that conference and in verse 18 he mentions James before he does Peter and John. And Paul shows deference, as do Peter and John, to James. It is

The Lord's Brother

James who presides, who rules the church, who is the overpowering personality. It is James who speaks with final authority. It is James who hands down the decree and it is James who covers that great horizon of the first Christian church. Why do I emphasize that so much? For one thing, because we do not realize it. For the second reason, if there was a hero in the first Christian church, it was James. It was not Simon Peter. It was James, the Lord's brother. He was a man of great stature in the church. You will run into him again and again. For example, Hegesippus, an early second-century historian, says that this man James was a holy man from his mother's womb. That would be Mary. From the day he was born he was a holy man of God. He drank no wine, he ate no flesh, and Hegesippus says that he prayed so much in the temple for his people that his knees were as camel's knees. I have come across this fact in my reading many times.

SECULAR REFERENCES

There is an apocryphal book entitled the "Martyrdom of James" and in that story the writer says that James infuriated Annas, the high priest and ruler of Jerusalem, by his preaching and that Annas had him thrown off the pinnacle of the temple and thus martyred him. Eusebius, who is the great historian of the third and fourth centuries, says that James, the Lord's brother, won the animosity and enmity of Annas by his preaching and that Annas had him stoned to death. Do you remember Vespasian? He was the great general of the Roman empire whose son Titus destroyed the temple, the nation, and the city. Eusebius infers that the judgments that came upon Jerusalem and Judah were due to the murder of this man, James the Just.

Finally, Josephus writes about James, and says that when Annas the high priest slew this godly man, it so infuriated the populace of Jerusalem that they deposed Annas and the governor of Jerusalem after a reign of only three months. I am just pointing out to you that this man James is the great personality of the first Christian century. Some have thought of John as the greatest apostle because of his writings in the New Testament. And because of tradition some think of Simon Peter. Actually, the tremendous character of the first Christian century is this man James, the Lord's brother. When the apostle Paul came back from his last missionary journey he reported to James, and did obeisance to his authority and personality. This is the

James, a servant of God, writing this letter to the twelve tribes of the diaspora.

THE LANGUAGE OF THE BOOK

Now, an amazing thing. The Greek of this letter is the finest in the New Testament with possibly Hebrews excepted. How was that? The Greek of James is like the pure, clear, simple English of John Bunyan in his *Pilgrim's Progress* or Daniel Defoe in his *Robinson Crusoe*. How is it that James writes such beautiful Greek? It could have been one of two things: first, he could have written through an amanuensis. You see, that is why 1 and 2 Peter are so different from each other. 1 Peter is beautiful Greek. 2 Peter is Greek as though the writer was looking up everything in a lexicon. 1 Peter is magnificent in the way it flows. 2 Peter moves along awkwardly. How could they be written by the same man? 1 Peter almost certainly was written through an amanuensis — Peter dictated it in Aramaic and then the secretary, the amanuensis, wrote it out in beautiful Greek. 2 Peter doubtless was written by the apostle himself, who was unfamiliar with the language. Both of them — the amanuensis and the apostle — were inspired of God. James could have written this epistle through an amanuensis or he could have written it himself. Being a great, mighty, noble man, and Greek being the universal language of the Roman empire, he could have written it himself. In any event, it is a strange thing that James should be written in the most beautiful words of the Greek tongue.

JAMES AND THE JEW

Now I would like to point out another amazing fact. James is the most Jewish book of all the books of the New Testament. For example, in James 2:2 we read: "For if there come unto your assembly a man. . . ." The word James uses is *synagogain*, "assembly," "synagogue." Look at verse 8. He refers to the royal law — the law of Moses. In verse 12 he refers to the law of Moses as the law of liberty. Look at verse 21. He refers to Abraham our father. Why, you would not do that. But James is a Jew, writing to Jews. In verse 23 he speaks of Abraham again, as the friend of God, and in verse 25 he makes another reference to the Old Testament — Rahab the innkeeper. This book is very Jewish.

OUR LORD AND THE JEW

Now I want to mention something that answers for me a question that often would rise in my heart concerning my Lord and His family — His people, Israel. You must bear in mind that I am very much of a persuasion, of a conviction. I am a premillennialist. That is, I believe in the literal interpretation of the Bible. When God makes a promise, I may not understand how God can bring it to pass, but I believe that in God's time, in God's day, in God's way every promise that God has made in the Bible will be fulfilled. At the consummation of the age, therefore, I believe God will bless Israel and God will use her mightily. If God does not do that, if He breaks His promises to the seed of Abraham, of Isaac, and of Jacob, I have no persuasion but that He also might break His promise to me and to you. So, I am a premillennialist. I believe in the literal return of our Lord. This same Jesus shall so come as we have seen Him go away. I believe that literally. I believe in the resurrection of the dead — this body. I think these very molecules and these very atoms will be quickened into life by the word and breath of God out of the dust of the ground, out of the depths of the sea. I believe in a literal resurrection.

I likewise believe in a literal kingdom. I think the Lord Jesus shall come to this earth and establish a reign in this planet and He shall preside over it and be King over it forever and ever. I believe in a new Jerusalem, a capital of this new kingdom of our Savior. I believe the streets of gold, the gates of pearl, the walls of jasper. When you read this book you will have to remember that I am of that persuasion. I believe in a literal translation, interpretation, meaning of the Word of God. Now, realizing that, let me point out to you an answer to something that used to bother me. We read in Zechariah 12, 13, and 14 this prophecy: "it shall come to pass that . . . I will pour upon the house of David and upon the inhabitants of Jerusalem, the spirit of grace and supplications. And they shall look upon me whom they have pierced, and they shall mourn for him, as one mourneth for his only son, and shall be in bitterness for him, as one that is in bitterness for his firstborn. In that day shall there be a great mourning in Jerusalem, as the mourning of Hadad-rimmon in the valley of Megiddon." This happened when the people cried and lamented over the death of good King Josiah. In that day there shall be a fountain open to the house of David and to the inhabitants of Jerusalem for sin and for uncleanness and "one shall say unto him, What are these wounds in thine hands? Then he shall answer, Those with which I was wounded in the house of my friends. . . . And his feet shall stand in that day, upon the Mount of Olives, which is before Jerusalem on the east. . . . And it shall be in that day, that living waters shall go out of Jerusalem . . . and the Lord shall be king over all the earth."

Now I believe that literally, just as the prophet said it. I think the Lord will appear to His people and He will show them His scars and the nail prints in His hands. They will be convicted and there will be a great repentance as the mourning when good King Josiah was slain by the armies of Pharaoh Necho at Armageddon. Now I believe that, just as it says here in the Bible.

And that introduces another question. Does that show favoritism to the Jewish people? The Lord is going to appear to them personally and there is going to be a great fountain of cleansing for them when they turn and accept the Lord in repentance. What about that? Well, that is what the Lord did with His family. And I am so glad. What a tragedy it would have been had the Savior returned to heaven and James and His brothers and His sisters were lost in unbelief. When the Lord died, He did not say to James, "James, take care of our mother." James did not believe in Him. But when the Lord died He said to John, "John, from now on, she is your mother." He said to His mother, "From now on mother, John is your son." And the Bible says that from that moment on John took Mary to his own home. Why did not Jesus commend His mother to James? Because James was not even there. James was an unbeliever. And had the Lord returned to heaven and left His own family in unbelief, it would have been of all things sad. Are you not glad that He won His family to Himself before He returned to heaven? He grew up with those brothers; He loved His family.

Now, in the New Testament the Lord called Israel My people, My brethren, and there has been no more traumatic thing in the drama of human story than Israel's rejection of her firstborn son. John 1:11 tells us that He came to His own and His own did not receive Him. What is John talking about? He is talking about Israel. He came to Israel and Israel refused Him. In Luke 19 it says that when the Lord came to the brow of Mount Olivet and looked over the city He wept over it.

Matthew 23 gives us some of the most scathing language in literature. "Woe unto you, scribes and Pharisees, hypocrites! for ye are like whited sepulchres . . . full of dead men's bones." How does that chapter close? It closes in lament: "O Jerusalem, Jerusalem . . . how often would I have gathered thy children together, even as a hen gathereth her chickens under her wings, and ye would not! Behold, your house is left unto you desolate." Christ was referring to the great judgment that came under Vespasian and Titus when the temple and the city and the nation were destroyed, and then He adds, "Ye shall not see me henceforth, till ye shall say, Blessed is he that cometh in the name of the Lord." There is a time coming when the Lord shall appear to His people, and they will in mourning and in repentance accept Him as their Savior and Messiah. Are you not glad? These people who have suffered so much, who have been driven into ghettos and into gas chambers and have perished by the millions, are you not glad that out of their unbelief, some day they shall look upon their Firstborn and receive Him as their Messiah, their Savior, and their Lord?

Dear reader, remember that conversion is always possible. A man may be hard, very hard, yet conversion is always possible. A whole nation may lie in refusal and rejection, but conversion is always possible. Revival is always possible. The greatest revival the world shall ever know by far, is in the Tribulation when God sends out 12,000 Jewish preachers from Reuben and 12,000 Jewish preachers from Gad and 12,000 Jewish preachers from Naphtali and 12,000 from Simeon and 12,000 from Judah and 12,000 from Levi — 144,000 Jewish converts preaching the gospel in the earth and John looking upon them said he had never seen such a throng in his life. Their robes had been washed and made clean in the blood of the Lamb. Revival is always possible. Miracles are always possible. Do not write off the presence and power of God. Do not think His arm is shortened, that He has not ability to save or that He is decimated in His almighty sovereignty. God is not done with us yet. There are other chapters that He is writing and they will be glorious and victorious and marvelous beyond what ear ever heard, what eye ever saw, or whatever has entered into the imagination of a man. We shall be blessed as we read James. It will be a strength and an encouragement for us all.

Chapter 2

TRIALS OF OUR FAITH
(James 1:2,3)

In our first chapter we introduced ourselves to James, the brother of the Lord. In his humility he calls himself a slave of Jesus, the Christ, but he is the brother of the Lord. And by far he towers over all the Christians of the first century. When we think of the Bible, we think in terms of the missionary, the apostle Paul, in terms of Simon Peter, the chief of the twelve. But had you lived back there in that first century, the great personality of the church at Jerusalem was its pastor, the brother of the Lord. All the others — Simon Peter, James, John, the other disciples, the apostles, Barnabas, and Paul — all showed great reverence for James. Now, having introduced ourselves to him and having seen who he is, it is of infinite blessing to read what he writes to the twelve tribes of the diaspora — his brethren scattered throughout the nations of the Roman empire.

Strengthen Each Other

After his greeting James writes: "My brethren, count it all joy when ye fall into divers temptations; knowing this, that the trying of your faith worketh patience. But let patience have her perfect work, that ye may be perfect and entire, wanting nothing." He writes, as you can see, as a pastor would. He writes as someone with a shepherd heart — "My brethren." The phrase is generically used to include all of the faithful. I might say it like this: "my brothers and sisters in Jesus." You see, we are taught to bear one another's burdens and thus fulfill the law of Christ. We are to comfort each other and strengthen each other, lest one of us should fall in despair. The Christian faith is one of

Trials of Our Faith

comfort and encouragement. We are to wipe the tears from one another's eyes. The Christian faith is not a vision, a dream of devils descending into hell. Rather, it is a vision and a dream of the angels ascending and descending on a ladder that leans against a shining throne of God. We may sow in tears, but we reap in joy.

THE FIERY TRIAL

So James begins with "my brothers and sisters in Jesus." Then he asks us to count it all joy when we fall into various "temptations." Let us look at that word *peirasmos*. In 1 Peter 4:12 we read the words: "Beloved, think it not strange concerning the fiery trial." There is that word — *peirasmos*. The word is translated here "fiery trial," which is to try you. Do not think it is some strange thing that has overwhelmed you. But be strong and rejoice in the fact that you are a partaker of Christ's suffering. Then when His glory will be revealed, you may be "glad also with exceeding joy."

Now, as we have mentioned, the word *peirasmos* here translated is "temptation," which is fine. But today the word temptation has a connotation of evil — you are tempted to do wrong. In our text, the word does not mean that. It means "trial," or "proving." It is the same as 1 Peter 4:12: "concerning the fiery trial — *peirasmos*." Once again, to confirm our understanding of that word, in Acts 20 the apostle Paul describes his three-year ministry at Ephesus when all Asia heard the word of the Lord. He describes his ministry by saying that he served the Lord with all humility of mind and with many tears and "trials" which befell him due to the plots of the enemies of the gospel.

So, let us take the word and translate it as James used it. "My brethren, count it all joy when ye fall into divers trials" — fiery trials. You see, all of us sometime, somewhere will be thrown into that burning crucible. If we have not been there already, it will be some other day and some other time. We all shall know of the fiery trials of the faith. This word *peirasmos,* trial, is not a sham word. Nor is it a spiritualization. It is a real word, describing a real and awful experience. These Christians to whom James has addressed the letter were being ground between the upper and the lower millstones of pagan religion and the persecution of emperor worship. They lived in the day of crucifixion, of the sword, of the fagot, and of the fire. The amphitheaters were consuming thousands of their number from one side of the Roman empire to the other. There was the cry to feed the Christians to the lions. It is no poetic word, this *peirasmos*. It was a real word of fiery, burning persecution and death.

Nor is it a word peculiar to that century and that day. Recently I had in my office at the church a man from Munich, Germany. He heads a group of dedicated men who are trying to get Christian literature beyond the Iron Curtain. He described for me the suffering, the martyrdom, the confiscation, the family destruction of our Christian brothers who live in Communist countries today. It is a harsh and terrible word — *peirasmos* — the fiery trial of those who commit themselves to the faith.

All in our day and in our time under God will suffer. It is a part of the purpose of God in allowing us to grow to maturity. We may not all have the same kind of trials. Ours may not be the kind of trials experienced in Communist countries. Ours may not be what others whom we know have to bear, but all of us shall know the burning of the crucible. James speaks of different trials, and we will all experience them. God tried Abraham when He told him to take his son of promise, Isaac, and offer him on a sacrificial altar. He was to take the dagger and plunge it into Isaac's heart, and let the rich, red crimson of life pour out. He was to do this to Isaac, his son, and the child of promise.

God, through our Lord Jesus Christ, tried the rich young ruler and told him to take all his wealth and to give it away — get rid of it. It stood between him and the kingdom. The young man had a trial — a civil war in his soul — and he debated it and went away with great sadness. The Lord Jesus told Simon Peter that Satan desired to have him so he could sift him as wheat — like a threshing machine. When you're converted, strengthen the brethren. Not every father will have a trial like Abraham. Not every affluent man will have a trial like the rich young ruler. And not every disciple of the Lord will be sifted like Simon Peter who denied that he even knew Christ. But we all are placed in that spot and all of us shall know the trials of the faith. These trials come suddenly — unannounced — unheralded. My brothers and sisters in Jesus, James writes, count it all joy when "ye fall into." We do not plan to, do not think to — it is a snare, a trap. It is similar to soldiers being ambushed. They are not prepared for it.

I think of Job. His sheep were grazing in the pasture. His sons and daughters were eating and drinking in the elder brother's house. The camels were in service and suddenly, without announcement, there came a howling wind from the wilderness and all of his children were slain. Then, lightning from heaven struck his flocks, and his herd and his cattle were burned up. Ravenous Sabeans came out of the desert and carried away everything that Job possessed. When one messenger came to tell him of the disaster of the wind, he had hardly spoken when on his heels came another messenger telling the disaster of the fire, and he had hardly spoken when the next messenger followed him with the disaster of the theft. What a trial — and Job was unprepared for it.

THE PURPOSE OF TRIALS

James writes of the heavenly purpose of trials. We must come to realize that it is the trying of our faith. *Hupomona* literally means "a bearing up under." The purpose of the trial is that it might work in us a bearing up under. In verse 3 it is translated "patience." You could translate it "fortitude," "enduring commitment." *Hupomona* is given that we might be *telios,* which is always translated in the New Testament as "perfect." We think perfection means being without sin, without moral turpitude. The word *telios* has no such connotation at all. The word means to reach the purpose for which God made the thing. A man would be a *telios* of a boy. He has matured — reached the purpose of his boyhood. An oak tree would be the *telios* of an acorn. As the *telios* grew to maturity, that was the achievement toward which it grew. That is what the word always means in the Bible. It never means sinless perfection. These fiery trials that come upon us are for the purpose of working in us a *hupomona* — an enduring commitment that we might be mature and strong in the Lord. So let us look at that for the moment.

God has intended that we have strength in our Christian character and strength comes to us in the trials that we endure. For example, a man grows strong muscles by strength and stress. He does this by lifting great weights. Any anatomical student will say that it is in stress, in pushing, in straining that our muscles are made. The same thing is true of our minds. It is in the discipline of study and concentration that a man's mind becomes sharp, knowledgeable, gifted. And so it is in our spiritual life. The trial that we face is a purpose of God that we might be strong, that we might be enduringly committed, that we might be mature, reaching that purpose for which God made us and saved us. I once read of a man who was watching a butterfly trying to escape from its cocoon in which it was born and imprisoned. The man thought he would help the butterfly so he took a sharp pen knife and slit the silk cocoon. And the little butterfly was free. It came out, flapped its wings feebly for a moment, then fell in exhaustion and death to the ground. God intended that the little creature find strength and maturity in striving, and when the striving was taken away it lived weakly and died sadly.

There is intent and purpose in what God does when He throws us into the crucible. In the ark of the covenant there were two typological things. One, there was a bowl of manna that had fed the people in the wilderness, and two, there was the rod that budded, and both of these have profound meaning for us. God has given them to us as lessons and types — food from heaven but ruled from heaven also.

The Manna and the Rod

The sustenance of life and the disciplines of life go together. The God who feeds us, who gives us manna from heaven is the same God who disciplines us, who uses the rod, who leads us into trial. You know, our problem is that often we cannot see the purpose. It is absolutely hidden from our eyes. God can see it, but we cannot. God knows why, but we do not. And when we are in the trial, it crushes us and we are in an agony because we do not understand.

A Modern Illustration

Some time ago a baby boy was born with a deformed foot. And as the lad grew that deformed foot became a severe handicap to the little fellow. His father, loving him very much, took the boy to doctor after doctor, and none could help. So he took the boy to this surgeon and to that surgeon and none could help. They gave him up. You know what the father did? He got many books on the subject and read and studied them. He learned about every bone in the foot. He studied every articulation — the tendons, the nerves, the muscles. And he made a strange-looking box with screws and felt washers at various angles. Then he took his son and put that deformed foot in that strange-looking box and tightened those screws. The little boy cried and the father tightened the screws until the boy was in agony. The father would come home from work in the evening and the little boy would cry to his father but the father would tightenthe screws. Day after day, week after week, month after month, when the father would come home from work the boy would cry in agony and the father would mingle his tears with the boy's as he tightened the screws. The day came when the father unloosed the screws, opened the box, and said to his son, "Son, stand up." And the boy stood erect for the first time. As the days passed the boy gained strength in his foot and he walked erect. There was no deformity. That boy grew to be a man and one day, over the grave of his father, he wept tears of gratitude and loving appreciation.

Maybe the father, being human, tightened a screw just one turn too much, but our heavenly Father never does — never. He knows exactly how much we can bear and He fits the cold north wind to the shorn lamb — not too much. He has a purpose in what He does. He means it for good. In these trials God has a way of purifying our motives. "Ha," says Satan. "Does Job serve God for nothing? No wonder he's good — you've hedged him on every side. You let me take away what he has and he will curse You to Your face." God in His permissive will said to Satan, "Take away everything that he has," and when Job saw all of his great fortune gone, even his children dead, he fell down before God and cried — "The Lord gave it all, and the Lord took it away. Naked came I from my mother's womb and naked shall I return there. Blessed be the name of the Lord."

Then Satan said to God, "You let me touch him and he'll curse You to Your face." The Lord said, "All right, only spare his life," so Satan afflicted him from the top of his head to the soul of his foot with boils — running sores, leprosy — and Job scraped himself with potsherds and sat in an ash heap, and in his misery cried, "Though he slay me, yet will I trust Him."

> When through fiery trials thy pathway shall lie,
> My grace all-sufficient shall be thy supply;
> The flame shall not hurt thee; I only design
> Thy dross to consume, and thy gold to refine.

Purifying our motives. Do I serve God for what I get out of it? Do I serve God for payment and reward, or do I serve God because I love Him alone? The trial purifies the gold of our motives. The trial brings to us the virtues of this life — of commitment and enduring love.

God's Will for Me

How often do I see that when the day comes, and the trial burns in the crucible, how often is there a tendency on the part of the sufferer to find fault with God. What have I done? Why is God treating me this way? And we war against God and fight against the sovereign, elective purpose of the Almighty. What a wonderful thing when I come to the place where I just receive it from God's hand, without bitterness, without word of reply or castigation or fault-finding or defiance. If this is God's will for me, then, Lord, let it be, let it be. If I lost my eyes, my hearing, my health, the dearest thing in my soul and heart and life, if it is God's will, if I go to the fiery furnace heated seven times, then, Lord, teach me the yielded, surrendered obedience that comes to those who bow in acquiescence before the sovereign God. Would it not be great to live a life of triumph like that? Nothing from the outside can destroy our inward peace and security and rest if someone curses us. In fact, we can bless in return. If someone despitefully uses us, we can love in return. No words of bitterness, just the grace and mercy and goodness of God. Lord, how can we learn to be thankful for the providences that come? God, instead of being defeated and in despair and sometimes bitter, how can we be grateful and thankful? Lord, how can I attain to such a grace, such a perfection?

I once heard of a man who, being desperately ill, was in a big ward in a charity hospital. And there was a custom in that ward that when a man was going to die they put a screen around him. So one day the nurse came into that ward, and, with helpers, put a screen around that man. When he looked at it he said, "O my God, I'm going to die. God, I'm a vile, lost sinner. O God, have mercy on my soul. Please, God, for Jesus' sake, save me. God, save me." And the Lord Jesus in His mercy reached down and touched that man's heart and brought him comfort and forgiveness and peace in Jesus. The nurse came and took the curtain away and said to him, "Sir, I'm so sorry. I apologize. I put the curtain around the wrong man. I ask you to forgive me." The man then exclaimed, "O nurse, it was the right one. It was the right one! Don't ask me to forgive you. It was the best thing that ever happened to me. Nurse, I found the Lord; I've been saved." The man began to shout and glorify God.

The Purpose and Blessing of Trials

That is the way it ought to be. For the time being our suffering may

Trials of Our Faith

mean death, it may look like death, it may look like terror, damnation, and hell. But God's purpose is to refine us, to save us, to bring us to Jesus. You know, I often think about that in national life. Our nation, affluent, with no cares, forgets God, and God has to come down and bring us to our knees; and it is on our knees that we find the Lord, strength, spiritual elevation, and maturity. I have heard it said that our generation could not go through a depression as my generation did, because they do not have the inward spiritual strength and stamina to bear it. That is what I have heard about America. You know, I have an answer for that. I think that if such a time came in the life of our nation, you would see more praying and more revival and more getting right with God and more going to church and more listening to the Word of the Lord than you ever heard in this generation past. That is God. Maybe we need it. If we do, Lord, grant that we will be brought to our knees and brought closer to You.

Let me mention one other thing — the blessing of the trial. When a man sits on an elevation, a mountain, and everything is going his way, he sees a certain thing, but when he sits on a mountain of trial and sorrow and tears he sees something altogether different. What does he see? I will show you. Moses is the son of Pharaoh's daughter, an heir apparent to the throne. He sits beside the greatest monarch of that civilized world, and is next in line to be king pharaoh of the land of Egypt, the greatest land in the world in that time. And what does he see? He sees affluence, rulership, all of the embellishments and accouterments of one who thus looks down upon a vast people. That is what he saw.

Now go with me to Mt. Nebo after forty years of fiery trial in the wandering in the wilderness. Moses is an old man. The Lord has prepared his sepulcher in Baal-peor. The Lord brings him to Pizgah's mountain height, to Mt. Nebo, and tells Moses to look. Moses lifts up his eyes to look and what does he see? He sees the Promised Land. He never saw that in Egypt. He saw that on Mt. Nebo.

So it is with us. In all of our comforts and affluences, and successes of life, we see certain things. But in the trials and sorrows and maybe in death, that is when we see the hills of glory, the beautiful city. That is when we see God's Promised Land. So James writes, " . . . count it all joy when you fall into trials."

Chapter 3

SEVEN TESTS OF FAITH
(James 1:1-3)

In our first two discussions on the Book of James we were introduced to him. He was the pastor of the church in Jerusalem and the great towering personality of the first Christian century. In this chapter we are going to take a glimpse at five chapters of the book, and we are going to do it in a certain way. We are going to see how James writes, what he says to us, and we are shaping it in the form of the seven tests of faith. James was a pastor, so we find him writing pragmatically, experientially. He does not write theologically; he is not a metaphysician; he's not a philosopher. But he is a pastor of the church and, as such, he will write about the common experiences of life. So he starts off by telling his brethren to count it all joy when they fall into various temptations. That may sound strange because temptation to us always carries an overtone of an invitation to evil, but it has no meaning like that here. The word *peirasmos* means to be tried, tested. Let me show you that in the Bible. In the story of the feeding of the 5,000 that we read about in John 6, John says that when Jesus lifted up His eyes and saw a great multitude He said to Philip, "Whence shall we buy bread, that these may eat?" (v.5). John tells us that Jesus said this to *peirasmos* Philip for He knew what He would do. The word *peirasmos* is used here to prove Philip, to test him, to try him. And that is the way the word is used in our text. It is not with an invitation to evil, not as temptation, but *peirasmos*, a trial, or a test.

Let me give an illustration. Many of you probably have seen a football game and you will have noticed that the coach sent in player after player. He did this to try them, prove them, test them. He had a large group of rookies on his team and he had to find out what they were made of and what they could do. That is *peirasmos*.

Recently one of the members of our church staff received his doctor of philosophy degree. But before he received his doctor's degree at NTSU, he had to go up there and endure a test. He had an oral examination — a *peirasmos*. And that is true for anyone who receives a degree. James says we should count it a joy when we fall into all kinds of trials or tests, proving us, for in the trying of our faith we are brought into the bearing up under — steadfastness and commitment.

Then he continues by saying that our weakness lies in our lack of wisdom, and if any of us lacks wisdom, he is to ask of God and God will not upbraid us, find fault with us — He gives to us liberally. In most any trial or test we need heavenly direction and God's wisdom — ask and God will not fault you for asking, but He will abundantly and gloriously answer. Then James says that our tests or trials sometimes are twofold. In verse 9 he speaks of the fact that they may be full of pleasure. In verse 10 sometimes they are full of pain. Sometimes (v. 9) they come of poverty, sometimes (v. 10) they come of prosperity. But we never escape the trial. You know, that is a strange thing. You would think that a man who had riches and success of fame or affluence would have no trial. Not so. The man who is successful, who is famous, who is rich, is tried just as much, though in a different way, as the man who lives in want. But James says blessed is the man who endures the trial, for when he is tried he shall receive the crown of life, which the Lord has promised to those who love Him.

Our Attitude Toward the Word of God

So, having introduced us to the idea of trials, pastor James speaks to us about our everyday life and the trials that we face in it. I picked out seven of them through the five chapters of his book. The first is our attitude toward the Word of God. Beginning at verse 19 and continuing through the rest of the first chapter, James talks about that attitude toward God's Word. "Wherefore, my beloved brethren (my brothers and sisters in Jesus), be swift to hear." He tells us to receive with meekness the ingrafted, implanted Word — the Word that we have been taught and the Word that we have heard preached, hear it, receive it, for it is able to save our souls. Then he speaks of the doing of the Word — "be ye doers of the word, and not hearers only." A doer of the Word shall be blessed indeed. So our first test lies in hearing and doing the Word of God. We first hear it, and that is the beginning of the Christian life. No man ever comes to the salvation of our Lord without the spoken Word. Simon Peter said we are born again by the Word of God. In James 1:18 the apostle says God begets us by His word. Paul wrote in Romans 10 that faith comes by hearing and hearing by the Word of God. It is a gift from heaven to hear unto the salvation of our souls. You know, man can come to a worship service and hear and hear, and one day he really hears. One day he really sees. This is the beginning of faith — hearing the Word of God, and then doing it.

James gives an illustration here, and it is an unusual one. He tells us to be doers of the Word and not hearers only, for, he says, a man who hears and does not do — that man — is as one who looks in a mirror and sees himself but does nothing about it. He just goes away and forgets what he looked at when he saw himself in the mirror. James likens the Word of God to the truth that a mirror will reflect. A mirror does not lie to you. It reflects you exactly as you are. And the Word of God does that too. We see ourselves as we are in the Word of the Lord. If we do not do anything about it, we are like the man who looks in the mirror and sees what he ought to do, but he does not do it — he just goes on and forgets about it. He looks in the mirror and notices he ought to shave, but he does not shave. He looks in the mirror and sees he needs a haircut, but he does not get his hair cut. Or a man's face is dirty but he does not wash his face. Two boys were talking and one said to the other, "I know what you had for breakfast this morning," and the other boy asked "What?" The first one informed the other one that he had eggs for breakfast that morning — "I see it on your face." The boy said, "I did not — that's what I had the morning before last." James uses a similar illustration about the Word of God.

Our Attitude Toward God's People

Now the second test the apostle writes of is our attitude toward God's people. He starts off as a pastor — "My brethren, have not the faith of our Lord Jesus Christ . . . with respect of persons. For if there come into your assembly . . . a poor man . . . and you say to the poor, Stand thou there, or sit here under my footstool," and you show favor to the rich man, you are wrong — it is sin. It is not right in God's house for us to have respect of persons, as between the poor and the rich or the known and the unknown. There is one place, James says, where all of us are equal before God. We all are sinners needing salvation. Whether we are successful or unsuccessful, whether rich or poor, whether learned or unlearned, we all need Christ. Did you know that almost all of God's people are ordinary, common people? Mark tells us that the common people heard Him gladly. In 1 Corinthians Paul tells us to look about us — not many mighty are saved. God's people for the most part are plain, ordinary people. I will tell you something else. I have never been in an assembly of preachers like an evangelistic conference, a convention, a convocation in which practically all of the ministers did not come out of poor and humble homes. A preacher who comes out of a rich and affluent home is scarce. And we may not say the poor people of the earth are unimportant. They are important. They are souls for whom Jesus died. And whether they are poor or not makes no difference in God's sight. Practically all of this world is poor. About half of it lives on the verge of starvation every day. And for us to have compassion, love, sympathy, and understanding for those who may not be as prosperous and as well off as some of us, for us to have that feeling of love and openhearted understanding, is pleasing to God.

OUR ATTITUDE TOWARD GOD'S WORK

The apostle speaks of our attitude toward God's work. "What doth it profit, my brethren, though a man say he hath faith, and have not works, can faith save him?" No, no. For when a man is saved, he is a different kind of man. This can be seen in all the facets of his life. It is in everything about him. He is someone else. He is a man of the Lord. And if there is no change, then the man has not found the Lord.

Sam Jones was a Southern preacher of the last century, a tremendously effective one. And being an evangelist, he went from place to place holding revival services. One day he was walking down a street and he saw a drunk in the gutter. A fellow walked by and told Sam to look. Sam Jones looked down in the gutter and saw the drunk. The man then said to Sam Jones, "Sam, that's one of your converts." Sam said, "That's right. He looks like one of mine. God had nothing to do with him." How true! "If any man be in Christ, he is a new creature:

old things are passed away; behold, all things are become new." A new heart, a new love, a new vision, a new dream, a new house, a new home, a new heart, a new life, a new fellowship. If a man has faith, it will reflect itself in the kind of a life he lives and the kind of deeds he does.

THE ATTITUDE OF OUR TONGUES, OUR TALK

The fourth test is of our talk, of our tongue, or our word. James tells us that the tongue is a dynamic, meaningful, and significant instrument, and he gives illustrations of it in his third chapter. He says that the tongue, though it is very little, is like the bit in a horse's mouth. It may be a big horse, but a little bit can turn him in any direction. He says the tongue is like the rudder on a ship — a great ship — but the ship can be guided by a small rudder. He also likens the tongue to a fire and what a great fire a little fire kindles. The tongue also is like an untamed animal. You can tame almost any kind of animal and James mentions some. But the tongue is hard for a man to tame. It is something only God can do. This tongue is the instrument by which we bless and praise God, and it also is an instrument that some men use to curse men. "My brethren, these things ought not so to be." "Out of the same mouth proceedeth blessing and cursing." Is not that a pragmatic, down-to-earth providence in which all of us share? Gossip is sometimes like a match that kindles a big fire. Just by saying "Did you know . . . ?" you can assassinate someone's character and ruin someone's life. James says that is unimaginable in the life of the Christian. How great a matter sometimes just a little fire kindles.

I once drove through one of the great national forests of Montana which had burned to the ground. It was a vast wilderness of waste. I asked the ranger what caused the destruction. He said that the flick of a cigarette had set it afire and had destroyed that whole great forest. Oh, what a little word sometimes can do. And instead of blessing God with our tongues, or words, sometimes we curse with those words. The same mouth can be used to praise God or to curse Him. When I was pastor in a little country church, each man in the assembly counted for so much. There were just a half a dozen of them. And one of those men I could never get to pray. I would call on him and he would always refuse. I ate dinner in his home and he did not say grace at the table. Well, being very young and foolish and falling into places that even angels would not dare to enter, I asked him why. He said this: "When I get angry, I am volatile in my spirit and I curse. When my team, as I'm plowing, doesn't do as I want them to do, I curse them. My boy hears me curse and, when you ask me to pray in public, in the church, my boy is there and I'm ashamed. When we eat dinner at the table, I don't say grace because my boy is there and he has heard me curse and I am ashamed." How sad. The tongue that could praise God uses His name in vain and curses. Recently a great leader in America lost the respect of the great mass of the American people when they learned how he talked when the world was not listening. It was sad and hurt your heart to know it. James says such a thing ought never to be. When a man speaks, let his yea be yea and his nay be nay, and he should never curse. Cursing is a sign of mental and moral weakness. If I look at a chimney that is propped up, I know that the chimney is weak. If I see a wall that is propped up, I know that the wall is weak. So, when a man speaks and he curses, I know that his speech, his thought, and his heart are morally and intellectually weak. Let your tongue be one of forthright honesty and integrity. Let its language and vocabulary praise God and bless men.

OUR ATTITUDE TOWARD THE WORLD

The fifth test is one of friendship with the world. "Know ye not that the friendship of the world is enmity with God?" Whoever would be a friend of the world is an enemy of God. What a strange and strong statement that is. But James is a pastor and I understand. In the last chapter of the last letter that the apostle Paul wrote, he said to Timothy, his son in the ministry, "Demas hath forsaken me, having loved this present world" (4:10). How many times I have grieved over that as a pastor. Here is a fine family, a dear couple, or a fine person and the world woos them away. They love the fashion of it and the entertainment of it and the appearance of it and the invitation of it. It is not long until the world is in their heart and they are lost to God.

OUR ATTITUDE TOWARD OUR WORK

The sixth test is our attitude toward our secular work and life. "Go to now, ye that say, Today or tomorrow we will go into such a city, and continue there a year, and buy and sell and get gain, whereas ye know not what shall be on the morrow." You should always say "I will do this and this in God's goodness and grace." We should remember the word of the Lord Jesus in Luke 19, where the Lord tells us to "Occupy till I come." Whatever I could gain is mine just for awhile. Then I leave it and someone else enters into it and possesses it. I am a steward, that is all, and my economy is what God places in my hand and I am to be faithful in it. I am to be a partner with the Lord in it. I think of some men who head great corporations, some who are great national figures. Think of what they could be if they just take God as a partner. And before they make decisions, ask their Partner about it. Some have accepted bribes or were involved in so many things that destroy corporations and integrity — think of what they could have been with God as a partner. Think of what a blessing it would be if a man would take God into his secular life. I think the Lord is interested in what you are doing. Ask Him about it. Pray about it. You have a decision to make? Ask your Partner. You have a commitment to make? Ask your Partner. You have an investment to make? Ask Him. You have a work that seems impossible, ask God — see what God does.

Our Attitude Toward Prayer

Our last test is our attitude toward prayer. "Is any among you afflicted? . . . Is any sick among you? Let him call for the elders of the church; and let them pray over him, anointing him with oil in the name of the Lord: And the prayer of faith shall save the sick, and the Lord shall raise him up; and if he have committed sins they shall be forgiven him." Look. What do we do when we are sick? James says we are to pray and to use means. Both of them — praying and using the oil. You know the Bible always does that, and never deviates from that. In the parable Jesus told of the good Samaritan, that poor man who had been robbed and left for dead, the priest passed by and the Levite passed by, and the good Samaritan came by and bound up the poor man's wounds, pouring in wine and oil. The alcohol was an anesthetic and antiseptic and the oil was a healing balm. Always that. Prayer and means. Prayer and the anointing oil. Not prayer alone. Both of them. That is why I believe in our physicians and pharmacists and all of the drugs and medicines. Who made penicillin? God did. Who gave us these healing chemicals and drugs? God did. And who gave us the mind to ferret them out and to use them? God did. Whenever you see a faith healer, tell him to go up and down the halls of a hospital. That is where he ought to be. He says he can heal, he should be there. That is where the sick people are. Heal them. Let us see him do it. Why would he not do it? Because he knows he is a fake. He knows it deep down inside, but he makes money on it — lots of money. He makes money off the illnesses of the people. God said we are to pray and use means. Pray, then ask God to give wisdom to the doctors — do both of these things. That pleases the Lord. And He says it is not only prayer for the sick, but also prayer for the sinner. Remember that he who converts a sinner from the error of his way shall save a soul from death and shall hide a multitude of sins. When we are sick, our attitude should be to take it to God. And to have a Christian physician is a benediction. Pray for the sick and pray for the lost.

One time a young doctor, who had just been converted, stood up and told the people that he was saved by the words of the preacher. Faith cometh by hearing. And — he made a gesture toward the senior doctor in the clinic — "I was saved by the prayers of this good doctor." Isn't that marvelous? "I was saved," said the young physician. "I was saved by the message of the pastor and the prayers of this good doctor." That is how God blesses. We try and pray, and God adds His benedictory remembrance.

CHAPTER 4

REAL RELIGION
(James 1:27)

We have come to the first of two chapters on the text: "Pure religion and undefiled before God and the Father is this, to visit the fatherless and widows in their affliction, and to keep himself unspotted from the world." Down-to-earth religion, real religion, pure religion, is to visit the fatherless and widows in their affliction and to keep oneself unspotted from the world. James is a pastor — he is the great overshadowing personality in the first Christian century — to whom Paul, Peter, and John paid deep deference. He is not a theologian. He is not a metaphysician. He is not a philosopher. He is a pragmatist. He is an experientialist, a pastor. And he writes according to the needs of the people. He has a shepherd's heart and he ministers to the people in Jerusalem. As such, he defines religion not in metaphysical or speculative terms, but as it is lived in our everyday life. Real religion is that which identifies with the people.

Where the People Are

It is a remarkable thing that the great social movements that have revolutionized society and changed the face of the earth are identified with people. You see it in their sign and symbol. Some years ago in a campaign for the presidency of the United States, a slogan of one of the parties was "A Full Dinner Pail — A Working Man's Bucket Full of Food." In the days of the '20s and '30s there was a movement called fascism. And its sign was a black shirt. Then there came a like movement, a totalitarian movement called the Nazi party, and its sign and symbol was a brown shirt — an ordinary workingman's shirt.

Real Religion

There is probably not a human being on the earth who is not familiar with the sign and symbol of the Communist party. It is a hammer and a sickle — an ordinary workingman's hammer and an ordinary sickle. All the movements are identified with people. But the problem we face so many times in religion is that the people generally relegate it to some other irrelevant world. They look upon it as something mysterious, something over and beyond us, unrelated, having nothing to do with our everyday life. Or else they define it in theological terms that have nothing to do with our common life. We inherited some of that from medieval scholastics. Some of their doctrinal discussions concerned how many angels could dance on the point of a needle. And so, in the world of theology, they look upon religion as something that is contained in a seminary, as a subject for dissertation and discussion, and which is found in dry, heavy tomes and vast libraries.

Not so, says the pastor of the church in Jerusalem. There is no doubt that there is mystery in religion. Wherever God is, He signs His name mystery. The fact that the world is created is mystery — inexplicable, unfathomable. If it is the word of God, it is supernatural. There is no doubt but that there is mystery in religion. There is no doubt but that theology is the backbone and strength of the religious faith. Without it, it turns to jelly. We would not scorn the theological definition, but James says that the mystery is not all there is to real religion. If you would know what real, down-to-earth religion is, says James, it is to visit the widow and orphan in their affliction and to keep oneself unspotted from the world. This is good for the pastor to remember and it is good for him as he leads the flock. This is God's definition. It is down here where the people are.

> A certain pastor of great austerity
> Climbed up in his high church steeple
> To be nearer God that he might hand
> God's word down to the people.
> He cried out from his steeple,
> "Where art Thou, Lord?"
> And the Lord replied,
> "I'm down here among My people."

Pure religion loves people — the lost, the unsought, the discouraged, the despairing, the weeping, the poor, the rich. It loves people — all of them. Our Lord was like that. He loved the poor. He had compassion on a man born blind. Jesus moved with compassion and opened his eyes. A man, bowed with an affliction for thirty-eight years, was at the Pool of Bethesda, waiting for the moving of the water that he might be healed. The Lord healed him. There was the widow, weeping over her only son who had died. The Lord stopped the funeral procession, raised up her only child, and gave the boy back into her loving arms. That is Jesus. One day He stopped at the foot of a tree and told Zacchaeus the rich publican, to come down for that day He would spend in his house. Real religion means saying to "the rich young ruler" that we love him. If his wealth separates him from God, invite him to get rid of it. Real religion knocks at the door.

Signs and Symbols of the Christian Faith

A little earlier I spoke of the signs and symbols of some modern revolutionary movements. Now let me speak of the signs and symbols of the Christian faith. The first, of course, is the cross. "God forbid," said Paul, "that I should glory, save in the cross of our Lord Jesus Christ." There are other symbols of the Christian faith.

Let me speak of some of them. When our church built Embree Hall, I was given the money to have six beautiful stained glass windows made. So we searched around and invited the finest company we could find to send their artist here to create those six windows. The artist came and I worked with him. Three of the windows on one side represented the old covenant, and the three on the other represented the new covenant. When the artist came to the third one on the side of the new covenant, I asked him if I could design it. He said, "I would love to see it." So I drew it for him. In the center I drew a medallion and in the medallion a picture of a church with a spire pointing toward God. I love to see a church with a great spire pointing toward heaven. On one side I drew a pair of clasped hands, and on the other side a hand knocking against the door. Underneath the clasped hand I put the word "Prayer" and underneath the hand knocking at the door, the word "Visitation." I did this with the thought and persuasion that the church is built up by prayer (intercession) and by visitation (knocking at the door). Pure religion, downright real religion before God and the Father is this — to visit — to knock at the door. This was the ministry of our Lord who from village to village and city to city and house to house invited men and

Real Religion

women to the faith, and this was the great ministry of the apostles.

There never was a more dynamic overturning of pagan culture and secular life than during Paul's ministry in Ephesus. All Asia turned toward the Lord. The seven churches of Asia were founded out of that ministry. The church at Colosse, Hierapolis, and the tremendous witness in Ephesus — how did Paul do that? He describes it in Acts 20. He called for the Ephesian elders and told them to watch and to remember that for three years he did not cease to "warn every one night and day with tears." He pleaded from house to house repentance toward God and faith toward our Lord Jesus Christ. Imagine that. For three years, day and night with tears, pleading repentance toward God and faith toward our Lord Jesus Christ from house to house. This is pure religion and undefiled before God and the Father. Not only is it to love people, not only to knock, but it also is a pleading in the name of Christ. It is presentation of our blessed Savior, testifying both to Jew and Greek, repentance toward God and faith toward our Lord Jesus Christ. It is coming, knocking, visiting. It is not a talking about the weather, though these amenities of life are always in order for conversation. Not about politics, though all of us are caught up in it, and not about the football game and baseball game, though so many are interested in it. Not about these things. These are casual, incidental, peripheral. The main topic should be, Do you know the Lord? Are you saved? No one can ever come to God unless he is saved. And there is one Savior — the Lord Jesus. He said no man can come to the Father but by Him. He is the way, the truth, the life. The only way a man can ever be saved, can ever see God's face and live, is through Jesus Christ, our intercessor and mediator.

Just As We Are — Through Christ

In the mornings I walk down Swiss Avenue where the parsonage is. I walk about a mile or a mile and a half. Way down the street there is a little black man. He has one eye and a big black patch where his other eye ought to be. He mows the lawn down there. When I pass by he always calls me by name and speaks to me cheerily. It does your heart good just to listen to that cheery voice call your name and speak to you. Recently I walked down Swiss Avenue and turned around to come back, and when I did my friend got in step with me and walked back up the street by my side. And he said, "Did you know that every

Sunday morning I hear you preach?" "Oh," I said, "I didn't know that." "Yes," he said, "I belong to the Church of God over here and I go to Sunday school, then I come home and listen to you preach." As he walked by my side I said, "So you go to Sunday school and then go home and hear me preach? Are you married?" "No." "Do you have any children?" "No." As we walked along he began to open up to me. He talked like a poor man talks. I know how that is, being brought up in a poor home in my childhood. Rich people seemed so big and mighty and so affluent. So he began to talk to me as a poor man talks. He said, "You know, I go to the office of the Chief of Police and sit out there and there's a receptionist in front of his office and that receptionist won't let me in. I just sit out there in that office, and along will come a rich man and he doesn't sit out there in that office. He just walks right on in, pays no attention to that receptionist, and he walks into the office of the Chief of Police and he just sits down. If the Chief of Police is not there, he just waits for him to come." And he said, "You know, when I go see the Sheriff I sits out there in that office and I just sits and that receptionist won't let me in. But along comes a rich man and he just walks by that receptionist into the Sheriff's office and just sits himself down. You know, when I go see the Mayor I sits out there in that office and the receptionist won't let me in and I just sits there and sits and along comes a rich man and he just walks right on in to the Mayor's office and he sits himself down in the Mayor's office." Then he said, "Do you know, some day we all gonna be up there before God and, you know, there ain't gonna be no poor and there ain't gonna be no rich up there in heaven. There ain't nobody going by that receptionist, whether he's rich or poor. He ain't gonna get by that receptionist to God." He said to me, "You know who that receptionist is? That receptionist is the Lord Jesus Christ. There ain't nobody that's going to see God unless first he goes with that receptionist. That receptionist is going to have to take him in and that receptionist is going to have to introduce and that receptionist is going to have to see you through. Nobody gets to God who doesn't go by, through, with that receptionist."

What a blessed thought — and what great theology.

CHAPTER 5

PERSONAL RELIGION
(James 1:27)

In our last chapter we looked at and discussed "Real Religion" and that is to visit the fatherless and the widows in their affliction. Now the second part of our discussion on that verse is entitled "Personal Religion." It is to keep oneself (in the King James version "himself") unspotted from the world. It is personal religion. It concerns a man in himself. When a man is in Christ he is not in the world. Others in the world have their heart there, their investments there. They have their hopes there, and when the world passes away every dream and vision collapses. But when a man is in Christ his hope is in Christ, his prayers and visions and dreams and life and treasure are in Christ.

Personal Religion in Our Church

Now, I am taking the text as just a subject, not an exposition. I would like to speak about religion that is personalized, that takes the form of flesh and blood — personal religion. We speak of it first in the church. Personal religion should be incarnate in the church. It should be religion with flesh and blood and life and breath. And in the church it should be seen first in the pastor. Why does not the pastor mimeograph his sermons and mail them out to the people? Because there is something about the personal presence of the pastor that cannot find any other substitute. There is nothing that will take the place of a man's word, heart to heart, eye to eye, soul to soul, when you look at him and hear his voice. Phillips Brooks, in his Yale lectures on preaching, gave the most famous definition of preaching that has ever been said by a man. To sum it up briefly, he said this: preaching is truth incarnate, expressed through a man's personality. Take the man away and you could write it in a book and mail it. Mimeograph it and send it out. But it is the personal presence of the pastor, looking at him, listening to his voice, watching him, that quickens the truth itself. The truth becomes embodied in him and he lives it out in the pulpit.

I now speak of personal religion, down-to-earth religion in the pew, in the people who come. The Scriptures say that our bodies are the temples of the Holy Spirit, so when we come to church we bring the Holy Spirit of God with us. And there's no other thing in the earth that can be substituted for the gathering of God's people in the name of the Lord. For us to be sensitive to those who are around us, makes the worship of God alive, quickened.

Recently I was talking to a couple of young men from the British Isles. They were from Spurgeon's College in London, so I asked them something about Spurgeon, the incomparable preacher of the Metropolitan Tabernacle in London. Spurgeon did not give an invitation when he finished preaching. All of his sermons concluded with an exultation of Christ and an appeal for men to give their hearts to Jesus, but he never gave opportunity for the people to come forward, to express their faith in the Lord. When Moody went to the British Isles and conducted those great crusades in the last century, Spurgeon loved him and admired him. They became close and fast friends. This was surprising because when Dwight L. Moody preached, not only did he make an appeal for Christ, but he also gave an invitation and asked the people to come forward and accept the Lord publicly and openly. So I asked the two young men how it was that Spurgeon, making an appeal for Christ, followed it through in encouraging the people to give their lives openly to the Lord, to be baptized, and to be numbered with the disciples of Jesus. The young men said it was like this. Spurgeon preached, yes. He preached the evangelistic message of Christ and he closed every sermon with an appeal for the Lord. But in that vast audience there were the members of the church who were sensitive to every visitor there, and when Spurgeon preached his message the convicting power of the Spirit of God moved upon the people. One man would be weeping and one would be kneeling and one would be asking God's mercy and one was plainly under conviction. When the sermon was done, the people of the congregation

Personal Religion

talked to those on whom the Spirit of conviction had fallen and they explained the way of salvation to them and personally won them to Jesus. Then they brought the new-found Christians, the new-born ones in Christ to the pastor, the pastor brought them before the deacons, and then in a church conference they were accepted into the fellowship of the church. When I listened to the young men describe that to me, I wondered if Spurgeon were to rise from the dead and preach as he did in London and give an appeal for Christ, would Christians of today be as sensitive to the visitor in their midst and to the one who was under conviction and be able to lead him to Jesus. I wonder what Spurgeon would find in the quality of our sensitivity, in our personal relationship to the Lord and to these who sit by our side in worship. I am afraid he would be disappointed in us, for we hardly have that close, personal relationship in our churches. Yet a cold, impersonal church is a monstrous anomaly in the kingdom of Christ. How can we know and love God and yet be insensitive to one another? He who would love God, let him love his brother also. I sometimes think that we are so impersonal in our faith — in our religion.

God came down to live in human flesh that we might know Him. What is God like? He is like Jesus, for God came down and took upon Himself the form and fashion of a man that we might know what God is like. He is the High Priest who can be touched with the feeling of our infirmities. So He tells us to come boldly to the throne of grace that we might find help in time of need. Jesus is incarnate that we might know Him and touch Him and that He might know us, and for us to be impersonal in the church is a travesty in the name of our Lord.

I now speak of personal religion in the house and in the home. Recently I was in Louisville, Kentucky, where I attended the Executive Committee Meeting of the Baptist World Alliance. The Executive Committee is divided up into smaller groups and I belong to a small committee that has to do with world reconciliation — we would say evangelism, the evangelization of the world. And in my committee were two members from Russia. One was a young woman named Volintina Rendena and the other was the minister of music of the Baptist church in Moscow. His name is Leonide Catchosfsky. It was a privilege to sit with them in that small group of about six or eight of us and listen to him when he gave his report from Russia. We were a small enough group so we could discuss some things I observed when I was in Russia. We talked about the ministry there in a world of official atheism and religious oppression. They cannot have revival meetings, they cannot have a Sunday school, they cannot print literature, they cannot distribute tracts, they cannot say anything in the way of a service or convocation outside of the church walls. How do they evangelize? The answer is that they do it in the home. Last year the church in Moscow baptized 128 — eighty percent of them were atheists. And they do their work under awesome oppression. They do it in the home. If they would invite two, five probably would come. If ten were invited, twenty might come. And they would stay all night long. They would listen to the message of Christ and to the teaching of the Bible.

Personal Religion in the Early Church

When I turn to the Word of God I find that same type of program was used in the early church. For example, in Romans Paul greets Priscilla and Aquila, "my helpers in Christ Jesus," and also greets "the church that is in their house." I turn to Colossians 4 and read, "Salute the brethren which are in Laodicea, and Nymphas, and the church which is in his house." I turn to the beginning of the Book of Philemon: "Paul, a prisoner of Jesus Christ, and Timothy our brother, unto Philemon our dearly beloved, and fellow-labourer, and to our beloved Apphia (who was apparently his wife). and Archippus (who apparently was their son), our fellow-soldier, and to the church in thy house." The greatest success and trial of the Christian faith ever known was in the first three Christian centuries. It literally subverted the civilized world. It swung the Roman empire on new hinges. It created a new civilization. There has never been anything like it in the history of mankind. And they did it without a church building. They did not build churches until about 300 years after Christ. You could ask these ancient, first-century Christians the same question that I asked that choir leader from the church in Moscow. How do you carry on your work? And the answer was, from house to house. If you were to ask the first-century Christians how they did it, they would answer, we did it in the home. We gathered friends and we gathered neighbors and there we taught the Word of God and we sang the songs of Zion and we prayed together.

I think this would be a good practice for us today too. We could invite those who do not attend church. I suppose some of you might hesitate and say, "I live in a poor home and our house is so humble." I know all about that for I grew up in a house like that. I remember that my mother took me from the farm to a little town so I could go to school because I had failed in my class the year before. I had failed because I was living too far away. My mother rented a little place — a poor place — so that I could go to school. I remember that so well. I was so small I hardly knew what it meant, but I remember the pastor of the church coming to see us. I sat down, just a little boy, by the side of my mother, and the pastor read a passage out of God's Book and knelt down there by our side and prayed. There are 10,000 things I have forgotten about my childhood, but I remember that godly man coming to that poor little place and kneeling down by our side and praying for us. That is personal religion. So do not worry about the condition of your home. I think God would love to come. I think Jesus would delight Himself to be there. And I think all who came would find help and encouragement for the way. It would deepen your spiritual lives. It would sanctify and hallow your homes.

PERSONAL RELIGION IN THE MARKETPLACE

I speak now of personal religion in the marketplace — out there where we work, where we live, where we walk. There is one thing about Jesus that never varies. You can never overexpose Him. You can talk about Him and talk about Him, but you cannot talk about Him too much. You can say endearing things about Him, and people can find fault with us for doing so. They can criticize the church and the establishment and say all kinds of things about religion, but it is hard to say things harsh about Jesus. Even Pilate said he found no fault in Him at all. Expose the Lord. Say a good word about Him. Recently a businessman came to me after the morning service and asked how it was possible to be the boss of the men and yet have that personal relationship with them? We are taught that if we are to be boss of the men, we must be impersonal with them and are not down where they are. We must keep ourselves separate. I told that businessman that that is typical of the world. Let me crack the whip and be harsh. Let me be the boss. You are dirt under my feet. You are over here, slave. That is the world. But I have learned this both from my reading and from my experiences that a man will work 10,000 times better for you if he loves you. Now, a man does not have to change his place from being a boss to get men to love him and to work for him. All who work know that we are in an organized society. The bank has to have a president. The corporation has to have a chairman. The fellow working on the road has to have a foreman. All of us realize that, but if the president is a fine man and the corporate chairman is a godly man and the boss is a Christian man, he can get his man to work for him. Saying a good word for Jesus — just reflecting on the Lord — is personal religion.

I was in a drug store recently looking for something among all those counters, when a big fellow came up to me and asked, "Aren't you Dr. Criswell?" I told him I was. He told me he had been to our church on occasion and had listened to me every Sunday on television. He then told me his story. He was a drunkard — an alcoholic. He said it was ruining his life and wondered if I could help him. Could I help him? There are thousands of people who need help. Could you help me? You see, (1) we must admit we are dying sinners. The wages of sin is death. I admit I am a dying sinner. (2) I must admit I cannot help myself. When the hour of my death comes, how am I to help myself? And how can I forgive my own sins? I must find help outside myself. (3) I can find it in Jesus. I can find it in the Lord. When I was without strength, in due time, Christ died for me, and (4) I can associate myself with the people of God. I can find strength in their presence. What if a man came down to your church to find strength and encouragement and you treated him as a stranger? Or the spirit of your church was full of divisiveness and quarrelsomeness and He came to find strength and help and encouragement? That is why James writes of personal religion. It is something that ought to live in me. It is the way I ought to be and it is something the people ought to feel in our presence. They should be constrained to love our blessed Lord. This is our appeal to you now. Open your heart to Christ and share your faith with others. Make your religion a personal religion.

CHAPTER 6

PAUL'S FAITH AND JAMES' WORKS
(James 2:14-26)

Let us look at the latter part of James 2. "What doth it profit, my brethren, though a man say he hath faith, and have not works? Can faith save him? If a brother or sister be naked, and destitute of daily food, and one of you say unto them, Depart in peace, be ye warmed and filled; notwithstanding ye give them not those things which are needful to the body; what doth it profit? Even so faith, if it hath not works, is dead, being alone. Yea, a man may say, Thou hast faith, and I have works: shew me thy faith without thy works, and I will shew thee my faith by my works. Thou believest that there is one God; thou doest well: the devils also believe, and tremble. But wilt thou know, O vain man, that faith without works is dead? Was not Abraham our father justified by works, when he had offered Isaac his son upon the altar? Seest thou how faith wrought with his works, and by works was faith made perfect? And the scripture was fulfilled which saith, Abraham believed God, and it was imputed unto him for righteousness: and he was called the Friend of God. Ye see then how that by works a man is justified, and not by faith only. Likewise also was not Rahab the harlot justified by works, when she had received the messengers, and had sent them out another way? For as the body without the spirit is dead, so faith without works is dead also."

Now let us look at Paul's discussion of the same subject. He uses the same illustrations, but comes apparently to a diametrically opposite conclusion. We read from Romans 4, "What shall we say then that Abraham our father, as pertaining to the flesh, hath found? For if Abraham were justified by works, he hath whereof to glory; but not before God. For what saith the scripture? Abraham believed God, and it was counted unto him for righteousness. Now to him that worketh is the reward not reckoned of grace, but of debt." (If a man works for you and you pay him, he worked for it. You owe it to him. You paid him a debt. Now to him who works for his salvation, no longer is it of grace, but of debt — God owes it to you and He just pays you what He owes.) "But to him that worketh not, but believeth on him that justifieth the ungodly, his faith is counted for righteousness" (vv. 1-5). And I add to that a typical verse from Paul in Galatians 2:16: "Knowing that a man is not justified by the works of the law, but by the faith of Jesus Christ, even we have believed in Jesus Christ that we might be justified by the faith of Christ, and not by the works of the law: for by the works of the law shall no flesh be justified."

THE SUPPOSED CONTRADICTION

I would suppose that the oldest of all of the supposed contradictions to be found in the Bible as the one you have just read. Some are disturbed by the fact that James says we are justified by works and Paul says we are justified by faith — and it cannot be both. So for the centuries this is a discrepancy to some. For example, the brilliant, able and dynamic Christian leader and theologian Martin Luther stressed justification by faith. His text was Romans 1:17, "The just shall live by faith." One day he was climbing up the steps to St. John's Church in Rome, on his knees, practicing good works that he might be acceptable to God. On the way up Romans 1:17 like a thunderbolt out of God's heaven hit his soul and his heart. He went home and nailed his ninety-five theses on the church door at Wittenberg and the Reformation was on. His text was, "The just shall live by faith," so he referred to this Epistle of James as an epistle of straw, and one unworthy to be included in the Word of God. That thinking is typical of the supposed discrepancy between the theological stance of James, the pastor of the church at Jerusalem, the Lord's brother, and Paul, the apostle to the Gentiles.

ABRAHAM AND FAITH AND WORKS

The message in this chapter concerns the truth that God reveals to us in these two apostles. First, let me point out that they are speaking of two different incidents in the life of Abraham. The apostle Paul is speaking of Abraham in Genesis 15, when Abraham came before the

Paul's Faith and James' Works 49

Lord and told Him that he was eighty-nine years old and God had not yet given him an heir. When Abraham was ninety-nine years old there still was no heir born in his home. Abraham reminded God that Eliezer of Damascus, his steward, was the heir in his house. God had promised Abraham a son in whose seed the world should be blessed, but no son has been given him and he was like a dried tree — the root had perished in his physical frame. He did not understand. Then God took His patriarch, Abraham, out under the heavens and told him to count the stars. Abraham said he could not — they were innumerable. Then God told him that so would his seed be that would come out of his loins. Now what would you think if God were to tell you that when you were ninety-nine years of age you would have a son? The Book says Abraham believed God and his faith was counted for righteousness. That is the way the apostle Paul says Abraham came into that conversion experience of regeneration. Before the right of circumcision — before Isaac was born or even Ishmael was born — God took Abraham's faith and made it for a righteous life to his account on that side of the ledger.

Now James is speaking of an altogether different incident in the life of Abraham. James is talking about Genesis 22 when the Lord told Abraham to take his son, the child of promise, Isaac, and go to a mount (Moriah) and there offer him up as a sacrifice to God. And Abraham took his son and bound him, and on the appointed mount, in the appointed place, in the appointed way, raised the knife to plunge it into Isaac's heart, believing that God would raise him from the dead. They are two different incidents. One, when without hope, Abraham trusted God for the promise, and the other, pointed out by James, when Abraham demonstrated and exhibited that hope by offering his son — his only son, the child of promise — before God in sacrifice. So, they are two different illustrations of the spiritual life in Christ, cited by these two apostles. The apostle Paul is speaking of that inner experience, when a man stands before God alone and trusts Jesus as Savior, and Abraham is a demonstration of that experience when he trusted God and God placed it on the ledger side for righteousness. James is talking about the outward demonstration when Abraham took his son and offered him openly as a sacrifice to God. So the two men are answering two different questions. Paul is answering the question as to how man can be justified in the sight of

God — how a sinner can be saved when he is lost and unholy and unrighteous — how a man can be declared holy and pure in the sight of God. James is talking about how a man's faith can be justified in the sight of men. How it can be demonstrated before his fellow humanity. Paul is talking about a man's faith in God's sight and James is talking about a man's faith in man's sight. They are two different things.

So, as we look at the vantage point of the discussion, we can easily see how each one follows through — the truth that God would teach us in the sacred Book. Paul is telling us how a man who is a sinner can be justified in the sight of God, can be accepted as righteous in the sight of God when he is not righteous. In Hebrews 12 it avows that without holiness no man shall see God. But no man has that character — no one of us is holy and pure. All have sinned and come short of the glory of God. There is none righteous, no, not one. Isaiah declares that our righteousnesses are as filthy rags in His sight. Even our prayers are not perfect. Our worship is not perfect; our thoughts are not perfect; our deeds and lives are not perfect, and without holiness no man can see God. Then how can a man be justified and stand in God's presence when he is unholy and impure? Paul says the only way a man can be saved and justified is by the grace of God. He must cast himself upon the mercies of the Lord. God had to do something for us, so He did. He made Jesus to be sin for us, that we might be made the righteousness of God in Him. For by grace are we saved through faith. It does not come of us, but of God and not of works. It is by faith and trust. Not of works, lest any man should say "I did it" — lest he should boast. In Psalm 51 David is crying to God after his grievous sin and he tells God that if He desired sacrifice, he would give it — offering, bullocks, calves, goats, sheep. But then he realized that "the sacrifices of God are a broken spirit: a broken and a contrite heart, O God, thou wilt not despise." That is, in his sin he cast himself upon the mercies of God. That is the only way a man can be saved. He cannot justify himself — he is not good enough; he is not holy enough. "Lord, be merciful to me, a sinner." That is the way a man is justified. The publican went down to his house justified, accepted as righteous, when he cast himself upon the mercy of God. That is the apostle Paul.

The Demonstration of Faith

Now James is talking from an altogether different vantage point.

James is talking down here. As a good pastor, he is addressing his words to men. Here is a man who has faith. Here is a saved man. How does he demonstrate that, justify that before men? He says here that faith without that justification, without works, is dead — it is sterile, being alone. Even as the body without the spirit is dead, so faith without works is dead. And he gives another illustration. If someone comes to you naked, and destitute, and hungry, and you tell him to go in peace, be warmed and filled, but you do not give him clothes to warm his body and you do not give him food for his hungry stomach, could that warm him and feed him? No! So the apostle James says that when we say we have faith, when we are converted, the only way that man can see the justification for our faith, the only demonstration of it is that they see it by the new life we live and the works we do.

Now, God does not need that. God knows our hearts and He sees into the deepest place in our hearts, so He does not need a demonstration of our works to know how we are in our hearts — whether or not we love God in our hearts, whether we have committed our lives to Him in faith or not. God does not need a demonstration, but we cannot see on the inside of the heart. All we can see is man's outward life. And if his life demonstrates and justifies his faith we can see it. If his life does not justify it, does not demonstrate it, does not exhibit it, then we cannot see it and the life of faith is dead.

One day two men came down the aisle in a revival meeting. One was named Jim and the other was named Joe. Years passed and one day the evangelist again saw the pastor and said to him, "You know, I remember that night when two men, Jim and Joe, came down the aisle and gave their lives to Jesus. How are they?" And the pastor replied, "Jim is a saint. Jim is a pillar in the church. He has grown in grace and is a strength in the house of God. Joe — Joe went back into sin after three weeks." Did that surprise God? No, for God knew all about it, since He saw on the inside of those hearts. God looked on the inside of the heart of Jim and saw a faith and a commitment that glorified Him, and the angels rejoiced. God also saw that Joe had just made a gesture — an outward profession — and it was not in his heart at all. God knew all of that, but the pastor did not know it. The evangelist did not know it. The people did not know it. It was only in works that it was proved Jim was justified by faith and it was only in works that it was proved Joe had no regenerated experience at all.

The only way you can demonstrate how it is in your life is by what you do. So the apostle James concludes that works make faith perfect.

The Need for Works in Faith

Let us discuss that thought for a few moments. The pastor of the church in Jerusalem looks out over his people and makes the statement that in works our faith is perfected. First, then, the Christian religion is something more than doctrinal rectitude. Somehow Christianity loses its heart, its very soul when it is defined as cold orthodoxy. I see that so often in ministers today. A minister may be doctrinally sound, fundamentally orthodox. He believes, preaches, and teaches the Word of God, but he is vindictive and forensic. He is unloving, and when you look at him and listen to him, you almost say you would rather be out in the world, for at least they are sympathetic and understanding of my sin or my fault. You would rather be there than with that man and his crowd, who are so censorious, critical, and condemnatory. I think I would rather be with those who are lost than to be with those who are so Pharisaical — holier than I. Is that the faith? Paul says no, no. Rectitude, doctrinally, ecclesiastically is not the spirit of Christ. You can be doctrinally sound and be very unloving and unkind, without the Spirit of the Lord. When I was in school we would turn the pages of history and would read about the dark ages, the medieval ages. We would read about those prelates and rulers of the church who could pronounce every shibboleth correctly, and they knew the ritual precisely. They conducted the services of worship in great and beautiful order. But their lives were despicable, and many were evil and vile men. Is that the Christian faith — to be orthodox, to be sound, to say every shibboleth and every word precisely, to know the ritual and to follow it exactly? No, says James. True faith is believing God and then exhibiting it before men.

May I point out another thing that James is saying to us? He says true faith in Christ is far more than metaphysical dispositions and philosophical dissertations. Somehow religion, the faith of Christ, is thrown into neutral when we juggle it around as having so many alternatives. The Christian faith was never meant to be strained thin in provincial philosophies. Let me say that I think it is a tragedy when Christianity is taken off the front pages of the headlines of the papers and placed in the theological discussions on the editorial page. God meant it to be headlined. It is Good News. It is the revolution that turns the world upside down or right side up. And when we make it theological, metaphysical, philosophical, psychological, sociological, ecclesiastical discussions, somehow it loses its drive and its sharp-pointed edge.

That is what the first Christians did. They took the faith out of the academy and placed it in the arena. They took it off the editorial pages and put it on the headlines of every newspaper. Let me remind you that while some of the apostles were still living, Ignatius was pastor of the church at Antioch. He was a mighty preacher, a man of God. He emptied the Greek temples; throngs of people came to church to hear him preach. He turned them aside from idolatry to the love and worship of the true God. And because of his dynamic effectiveness, he was brought before the Roman Caesar, who sentenced him to be exposed to the lions in the colosseum. I have read it many times in books of history that when Ignatius stood in the arena and they opened the cages for the wild beasts, he held out his hand to the leading lion and above the sound of the crunching of bones he was heard to say, "Now I begin to be a Christian." The demonstration of it is the justification of the faith. Not on the editorial page in a discussion, but on a headline — what God's people are doing.

THE ROLL CALL OF FAITH

Hebrews 11, one of the greatest chapters in the Bible, is called the Faith Chapter — the roll call of the heroes of faith. Remember how it reads? "By faith Noah." How do you know "by faith Noah"? When God told him He would destroy this world in a deluge in 120 years, Noah believed God with a hammer and saw and timbers and an ark. That is the faith. "By faith Abraham." How do you know by faith Abraham? When God called him to go out to receive a country he should afterward have for an inheritance, he went out, knowing not whither he went. That is the faith. "By faith Moses." How do you know by faith Moses? When God called him he forsook the throne of Egypt, choosing rather to suffer affliction with the people of God than to enjoy the pleasures of sin for a season. He renounced the throne of Egypt that he might be identified with the suffering slaves of God. That is the faith. "By faith Rahab." What do you mean by faith Rahab? She took the scarlet line. Rahab the innkeeper placed a scarlet line in the window, gathered her family, and waited for the deliverance of the Lord. That is the faith. It is always those two. It is the commitment in trust and the commitment in deed. Take up your cross, the Lord says, and come and follow Me. Give your life to Me and follow Me. The lift and the load — the burden and the blessing. And they are always together.

Once there was an oriental traveler carrying a suitcase and he called for a coolie. The Japanese runner had a long pole on his shoulder with a sling on one end and a sling on the other. He took the man's suitcase and put it in one sling and he took a rock, about the weight of the suitcase, and put it in the other sling, and balanced the pole on his shoulder and went trotting away. He doubled the burden, but he made it light. That is exactly the way God does with us. There is a load and a lift — there is a burden and a blessing. There is a faith and there is a work. And when we do both of them together, Paul and James, we are infinitely blessed. The world is blessed and the name of Christ is honored.

CHAPTER 7

ORTHODOXY OF THE DEVIL
(James 2:19)

In our last chapter we discussed the second half of the second chapter of James. Now we are going to take a look at the 19th verse. James is writing about those who say they have faith, but they do not demonstrate it. They are not incarnate in it. They just say it, but it is not a part of their life. So he says, verse 19: "Thou believest that there is one God; thou doest well: the devils also believe, and tremble." That is an interesting avowal he makes. The devils — *daimonia* actually demons — there is just one *diabolia*, just one devil, just one Lucifer, just one Satan, and he presides over a fallen kingdom of *daimonia* — demons. And they all — Satan and his legions — believe that there is a God. One God. James uses another expression here that forcefully says they not only believe, but they also *frissousin*. It is the only place the word is used in the Bible. In Latin the word is *parao*. And when we take the Latin word in English, we spell it *horror*. Both words, whether in Greek or Latin, mean "standing straight up." It refers to a man's hair when he is frightened out of his wits and his hair stands straight up. The word here refers to a hair standing straight up out of terror. Here it is translated "tremble," "quaking." It actually means extreme fear. The devils believe and, knowing what is true, they are terrified in extreme and agonizing fear. Is that not a strange thing about evil? You would think that with all of the agony people who live criminal lives go through, they would change. I do not suppose there ever lived a man who went through as many horrors as did Dillinger. He even had the tips of his fingers cut off in order to destroy the identifying marks of his fingerprints. He lived a life of horror, and yet he became more criminal every day that he lived. Why did he not change? Why does the devil not change? Or maybe I should say why don't we change? Somehow it just does not work that way.

The Distinction

And that leads me to a discussion of orthodoxy and change, regeneration, salvation. It is necessary that we be able to distinguish between the devils and the saints. Pragmatically, it is vital to us in the house of God. A church is an *ecclesia*, a called out, redeemed people of the Lord. That means if we are called out, we are separated from someone, and it is necessary that we be able to distinguish in that separation. This is not a new teaching for Jesus taught us that. In Matthew 7, in the Sermon on the Mount, our Lord asked, "Do men gather grapes of thorns, or figs of thistles? . . . By their fruits ye shall know them." A pastor was discussing the work and assignments of his members when a listener said to him, "Pastor, you're judging, and you ought not to judge." The pastor replied, "I'm not judging; I'm just fruit inspecting." And that is what we have to do in the church — in the choice of teachers, deacons, leaders, there has to be that decision made — a distinction between the devils and the saints.

Not only did Jesus teach us that, but the apostle Paul enforced it in 2 Corinthians 6. Paul writes, "Be ye not unequally yoked together with unbelievers; for what fellowship hath . . . light with darkness? . . . Wherefore come out from among them, and be ye separate, saith the Lord, . . . and I will be a Father unto you, and ye shall be my sons and daughters." Now, sometimes that distinction is easy to make. For example, in 1 John the apostle writes, "They went out from us, but they were not of us; for if they had been of us, they would no doubt have continued with us: but they went out, that they might be made manifest that they were not all of us" (2:19). Now that is plain and simple. People who are not regenerated are not Christians. They soon fall away and go back into the world. And when that happens, the difference between the child of God and the child of unbelief is manifest. But it is not always that way. Sometimes the line of demarcation between the devils and the saints turns gray and it is hard to make that distinguishment. Do you remember in Acts 8 when Phillip was in Samaria and had that tremendous revival meeting? The Bible tells us that Simon Magus believed and was baptized. When Simon

Magus saw the wonderful, miraculous works wrought under the hand of Simon Peter by the gift of the Holy Spirit, he sought to buy the gift of the Spirit with money. That is where we get the word "simony." Simony refers to buying places in the church with money, especially in the days when they would sell the office of a bishop or auction the office of a cardinal. When Simon Magus tried to buy the Holy Spirit Peter said to him words of denunciation that are bitter and deep. You did not know what kind of a man Simon was until he tried to buy the Holy Spirit with filthy lucre. And you still do not know how it is with some people today. It is hard to know the devil from the saints. In 2 Corinthians 11 Satan is called an angel of light, and it is hard to distinguish him. Any time you see the devil depicted as a being with a red suit, horns, a forked tail and a pitchfork, that is a caricature. Satan likes that because it hides his face. This is what we may think he is, but he is not that way at all. He is described as an angel of light. He is brilliant and attractive. He is persuasive and orthodox. He is doctrinally correct.

The Necessity of Repentance

Imagine this scene. Satan walks down the aisle of my church some Sunday, and says, "Dr. Criswell, I want to join the First Baptist Church in Dallas. It's a great congregation and I want to belong to it." So I say, "Well, this is amazing, surprising — the devil wants to join the church." But I ask him some questions first, and listen to his brilliant testimony. I ask, "Do you believe that Jesus is the Son of God?" "I certainly do. Why," says the devil, "you got me down wrong in the fourth chapter of Matthew. It says there that you have me saying, '*If* You are the Son of God, turn these stones into bread. *If* You are the Son of God, cast Yourself down from the pinnacle,' and you make it a conditional, a subjunctive. It's not. It's indicative. What I said was, and it is written in the book if you'd just translate it correctly, '*Since* You are the Son of God, make the stones into bread. Since You are the Son of God, throw Yourself down.' No," says the devil, "they wrote me down wrong there. I believe Jesus is the Son of God. I've known Him from before the foundation of the world. I knew Him in heaven. I knew Him before He was incarnate. I certainly believe that He is the Son of God."

"Well, do you believe He is born of a virgin?" "I certainly do. I saw the angel make the glorious announcement to the virgin Mary and I was there in Bethlehem when He was born. I saw the star and I heard the angels sing. I believe in the virgin birth."

So I say, "Do you believe Jesus died on the cross?"

"Yes sir, I was there."

"Well, do you believe that He was raised from the dead?"

"Yes sir, I was there. I saw the stone rolled away. I saw the Roman seals broken; I saw Him step out. I was there."

"Well, do you believe that He's coming again?"

"I do. The apostle John wrote of me in the apocalypse that I had a short time. I believe."

"Well, I'm a Baptist pastor. Do you believe in being baptized? Do you believe in immersion?"

"I certainly do. I was at the Jordan River, and I saw John the Baptist baptize Jesus. I'll make you a good Baptist," says the devil.

"Well, I have another question to ask you, Mr. Devil. You say you want to join this church? Will you come, will you be present?"

"Oh," he says, "I'll be there every service. I won't miss a one. I'll stand right by the side of the pastor. In fact, I'll join the choir. I'll get into the members themselves. I'll be a good deacon for you. I'll go to all the deacons' meetings. I won't miss a one. I'll be right there."

Well, with a testimony like that, I make a motion that we take him in. And someone seconds the motion. All in favor say "Aye" and hold up your hand. Amen. It's unanimous. We have him in the church and he is just as orthodox as he can be. He believes every article of the faith. He does not doubt any of it.

However, there is one other question to ask him — just one. "Satan, you have walked up and down the earth oversowing God's fields with tares, breaking many hearts. You have afflicted children, you have destroyed homes, you have ruined lives. Satan, have you repented? Have you turned? Have you changed and do you open your heart to accept Jesus as your Savior? Do you bow down and worship Him as the Lord of Life? Do you? Will you?" And we all know what his answer would be.

You Must Be Born Again

That imagined scene reminds us that we cannot have the Christian faith without that change of life — being born from above. Just as you cannot have rain without water, just as you cannot have the sun without energy and light and heat, just as you cannot have steel without iron, so you cannot have a man without a soul in him, for man is a living soul. So it is you cannot be a redeemed child of God without a new heart, a new love, a new commitment, a new godwardness. A man can have an intellectual assent in his attitude toward the Christian faith. He can believe every article of the doctrine — all of it. He can accept the Bible as the Word of God. He can believe that all the miracles came to pass and believe that Jesus is the Son of God. Some of the most intellectual professors in the earth are men trained in theology, but they are not saved — they are not regenerated. They do not know Christ as the Lord, the Savior, the Redeemer. It has to be more than intellectual assent. The devil believes, but he is not saved. We can have a social experience in the circle of the church. We can be pulled into it in a social way, through friends or through family members.

In John 6, the Lord said to that multitude following Him that they were following Him because they ate of the loaves and were filled. In the Orient they have what they call "rice Christians." They come to the church and associate themselves with the church because they eat from the hands of the missionaries. We can be pulled into the church socially. We join it because of the family or because of friendship or some other reason.

Emotion and Our Faith

Another way that we can have an experience in religion is emotionally. Now I am the last one in the world to discount feeling in religion. I think when you take emotion out of human life we become clods, and it is because we have taken emotion out of religion that we see some things happening today. Here is one thing — people find their emotional responses and happinesses outside of the church. They will go to a cheap movie and cry over some sorry melodrama, or they will go to the Cotton Bowl and yell their lungs out.

I will tell you another thing that comes out of the emptying of emotion in religion. That is the charismatic movement. The charismatic movement is a response of people against the dry ritual they find in the church. Their hearts are hungry — their lives are hungry and God made us that way. Love is an emotion as well as a dedication. Patriotism is an emotion. The great moving forces we know and love are emotional and yet it is not just emotional. It is something more.

On Palm Sunday when the Lord rode into Jerusalem, the people shouted "Hosanna to the Son of David: Blessed is he that cometh in the name of the Lord; Hosanna in the highest." They took off their garments and put them on the street where the animals could walk over them. They took palm branches and placed them in front of the Lord as He entered, and they waved the palm branches in the air. They were emotionally up that day. You know, some of the same people, that following Friday, before the courthouse of Pontius Pilate cried, "Crucify Him, away with Him. It isn't fit that such a man walk on the face of the earth." Emotions are like this and that. They go up and down. And if you ever tie your religious faith to emotion, it will drag you to death. One day you will say, "Glory, I'm saved. I can hear the angels sing. I can see the courts of heaven. O glory, I'm saved." Then the next day you may say, "You know, I'm not really regenerated. I really don't know the Lord. I'm not a Christian." And all because the feeling has ebbed away. All feeling is that way — it rises and falls. Even love is that way. A man said he loved his wife so much one day he could eat her up, and the next day he wished he had done it! That is just typical. You are not going to stay up high — on anything. It just does not work that way. Feelings rise and fall. That is, if you are normal. If you stay down all the time, you are afflicted with melancholia. If you are up all the time, you are an idiot. If you are normal, you go up and down, up and down.

In Matthew 12 our Lord tells a little parabolic story that is pungent and true. He tells of a man who had an unclean spirit and the unclean spirit was pushed out of him — cast out of him. The unclean spirit went around, trying to find rest and could not. He then took seven other spirits worse than himself, came back, dwelt in that man, and his last day was worse than the first. There are men today with unclean spirits. They are full of lust or cursing or volitive badness or get drunk. So one of them says he is going to do better, and the first day of January he makes a New Year's resolution, and resolves to cast out those evil spirits in his heart. He is not going to curse anymore, he is not going to lie anymore, not going to be bad anymore — he is going to be good. And for awhile he does just fine. Through the 15th of January, maybe the 1st of February. Then after that he goes back into that old life and he is worse than he ever was. Why? Because he was not regenerated. His heart was empty. He reformed, but he did not fill his heart with the Spirit of God. So all those evil spirits came back and he was worse than he ever was. Salvation is more than reformation.

Then what is it? The apostle Paul, in describing his ministry in the Asian city of Ephesus, said in Acts 20:31, that for three years he "ceased not to warn every one night and day with tears." Preaching repentance toward God and faith toward our Lord Jesus Christ. What is the Christian faith? What is redemption? What is regeneration? What is it to be saved? What is salvation? It is this. In my heart of hearts I turn. I have been going that way, now I am going this way. It is a turning — repentance means a change of mind, or direction. It is turning, the turning Naaman had to make. When Elisha told him to wash in the muddy Jordan seven times in order to be healed of his leprosy, he drove his chariot away from Elisha's home in anger. His servant told him to obey Elisha, to "wash and be clean," so Naaman had to turn his chariot around, go down to the Jordan and dip himself in that water seven times. And when he came up the seventh time, his flesh was like the flesh of a little child, and he was clean. It is a turning. It is an acceptance of Christ as Savior. It is an opening of the heart, the life, the soul to the blessedness of Jesus. It is a bowing down before our Lord. I accept Him for all that He said He was. I believe He is able to do all that He promised. I even believe He could raise me from the dead. Though I die, yet in my flesh shall I see God. I believe He will stand by me in the hour of my death. I believe He will be my lawyer, my mediator, my counsel in the day of judgment. I believe He is able to forgive me all my sins and to see me through. That makes me a Christian, a child of God, a member of the household of God.

Chapter 8

THE UNTAMED TONGUE
(James 3:1-12)

In our preaching through the Epistle of James, we have come to the third chapter, and the title of this chapter is, "The Untamed Tongue." The pastor writes, "My brethren . . . If any man offend not in word, the same is a perfect man, and able also to bridle the whole body. Behold, we put bits in the horses' mouths, that they may obey us; and we turn about their whole body. Behold also the ships, which though they be so great, and are driven of fierce winds, yet are they turned about with a very small helm, whithersoever the governor listeth. Even so the tongue is a little member, and boasteth great things. Behold, how great a matter a little fire kindleth! And the tongue is a fire, a world of iniquity: so is the tongue among our members, that it defileth the whole body, and setteth on fire the course of nature; and it is set on fire of hell. For every kind of beasts, and of birds, and of serpents, and of things in the sea, is tamed, and hath been tamed of mankind: But the tongue can no man tame; it is an unruly evil, full of deadly poison. Therewith bless we God, even the Father; and therewith curse we men, which are made after the similitude of God. Out of the same mouth proceedeth blessing and cursing. My brethren, these things ought not so to be. Doth a fountain send forth at the same place sweet water and bitter? Can the fig tree, my brethren, bear olive berries? either a vine figs? so can no fountain both yield salt water and fresh." This is very practical and down-to-earth discussion about our works and what we say.

The Lord God assigns the development of different aspects of spiritual truth to different apostles. For example, He gave to the apostle Paul the assignment by inspiration to develop the truth of justification by faith. We are saved by grace and not by our works. He gave the author of Hebrews the assignment of developing the doctrine of the atonement of Christ and His High Priesthood. He gave to John the assignment of developing the doctrine of the deity of our Lord and the love of God. Likewise, the same Holy Spirit assigned to James, the Lord's brother, and the pastor of the church at Jerusalem, this assignment to develop the practical aspects of the Christian faith — our moral rectitude in living the Christian life. James was a man of singular and unusual integrity. In secular history he is called James the Just, the only man of the New Testament I know of who is described and presented in secular history. He writes under inspiration of the practicalities of the Christian life, and one he discusses is the one about our tongue.

The Importance of Words

James says that our history, our lives, and our destiny are changed by our words. He gives us an illustration. A giant horse is turned around with a little bit in the mouth. A tremendous ship is guided by a little rudder, a little helm. A vast conflagration is set afire by a little spark. How big a matter a little fire, a little spark, will kindle. Then he describes how the tongue can be used to destroy and to poison. He says the tongue can be an unruly evil full of deadly poison. There are many people who have never set fire to a man burned at the stake, they have never clapped their hands at the shrieks of those who in agony were being torn apart by a ferocious lion in some colosseum. There are people who have never beat the drums to drown out the agonizing cry of those who were offered to the fiery god of Moloch, but there are people without number who assassinate friends, neighbors, and acquaintances by untrue tale bearing, vicious and evil words. Sometimes just by the arching of an eyebrow, or a sneer from the lips, or a shrug of the shoulders we hurt and destroy. I do not think there is anyone of us but has felt the sting of unkind words.

There was a godly Quaker who came up to her pastor and said, "Pastor, I would think and dost thou not also think, that if one lived beautifully, and walked correctly, and stayed away from evil that others seeing us would be inclined to love our religion?" And the pastor replied, "Sister, if thee covered thyself with a coat of feathers white as the driven snow, and if thee had a pair of wings as shiny as those of the angel Gabriel, on this footstool of the earth there would be somebody, somewhere so color-blind as to shoot thee for a blackbird." You cannot get away from the unkind word. All of us have felt it and the sting and the hurt of it. Sometimes, it can be disastrous. With that tongue, he says, "we bless God" and with the same tongue, we curse men who "are made after the similitude of God."

The Importance of Good Words

How tragic that with the same voice, and the same words, and the same tongue by which we approach the throne of Grace we also hurt men, sometimes almost irrevocably. Why do you do that? Why do I? I take a leaf out of my life of which I am abjectly ashamed. One day a man came to the parsonage of the church in Dallas. When I sought to detain him he said, "No, I am going to see so-and-so. He once was a preacher and he has fallen into lots of troubles, and I'm going to see him." I said, "That's right. He has fallen into lots of trouble." Then I purposed to repeat to that man the sordid tales of how the former preacher fell out of the ministry and ruined his life. He, not knowing that I was getting ready to repeat a tale, interrupted me and said, "Yes, he has lots of troubles and he is sick now and I'm going to see him. For you see," he said to me, "he's the man who won me to Christ." He said, "Nobody paid any attention to me, nobody ever sought me out, nobody ever invited me to the Lord, but he did, and I have loved him ever since. He won me to Christ and I'm going to see him. He needs me, he's in trouble, and he's sick." The man went on his way and I bowed my head. I felt so wrong, and so unclean. What good would it have done for me to repeat the tale that took him out of the ministry and destroyed his life. I felt dirty and unclean, and when I think of it, I think of it with shame.

> If you see a tall fellow ahead of the crowd,
> A leader of the group marching fearless and proud;
> And you know of a tale whose mere telling aloud
> Would cause his proud head in anguish be bowed,
> It's a pretty good plan to forget it.
>
> If you know of a skeleton hidden away
> In a closet guarded and kept from the day,
> In the dark, whose showing, whose sudden display
> Would cause grief and sorrow and lifelong dismay,
> It's a pretty good plan to forget it.

> If you know of a spot in the life of a friend,
> We all have spots concealed world without end,
> Whose touching his heartstrings would hurt or rend
> Til the shame of its showing no grieving could mend,
> It's a pretty good plan to forget it.
>
> If you know of a thing that will darken joy
> Of a man or a woman, a girl or a boy;
> That will wipe out a smile or the least may annoy
> The fellow or cause any gladness to cloy,
> It's a pretty good plan to forget it.

The Tragedy of Bad Words

If I cannot say something good let me say nothing at all. For God has set us in the world to encourage, to be a blessing, to help.

Now the inspired pastor of the church writes of the effects of our words that hurt. He says that it hurts the person who says them. "The tongue is a fire . . . and it defileth the whole body . . . and it is set on fire of hell." When I repeat a sordid tale, or when I magnify a falsehood, or when I use words that hurt, it does something to me. It defiles the whole body. It has an effect on my personality. When a good-looking boy, or a beautiful girl uses bad language and tell tales he or she immediately becomes unclean and unattractive. Evil words defile the whole body — my mind, my heart, my soul, my well being. They hurt.

Do you remember those three little monkeys? One has his eyes covered — see no evil. One has his mouth covered — speak no evil. And one has his ears covered — hear no evil. The whole body.

> A gossipy tongue is a dangerous thing
> If its owner is evil at heart.
> He can give whom he chooses many a sting
> That will woefully linger and smart.
> But the gossipy tongue would be balked in its plan
> For causing heartburning and tears,
> If it weren't helped out by the misguided man
> Who possesses two gossipy ears.

The whole body is involved and the whole body is defiled when we use our tongue and our words to hurt, and not to bless.

John tells us that the tongue is uncontrollable. We can tame the birds and the serpents and the animals in the sea. You can tame and train almost anything, but the tongue when it gives itself to words of hurt are beyond recovery, beyond taming. It is uncontrollable.

A woman repeated a tale on another woman. It brought that other woman misery and agony. It was found later that the tale was not true and the woman who bore it and scattered it abroad went to a sage and asked, "What shall I do?" The sage said, "Take a pillow of feathers and scatter them over the town." So she took a pillow of feathers and scattered them up and down the streets of the city and then came back to the sage and asked, "Now what shall I do?" The sage then told her to "Gather them all up again." And she replied, "The wind has blown them all over. I could never find them again." Then he said, "Nor can you ever gather back all of those words you said." When I say it I cannot pull it back. I cannot unsay it, nor can I make atonement for the hurt that it has done.

Good Words for Jesus

James closes with the thought that with the tongue "bless we God . . . and therewith curse we men. . . . Out of the same mouth proceedeth blessing and cursing. My brethren, these things ought not so to be. Doth a fountain send forth at the same place sweet water and bitter? Can the fig tree, my brethren, bear olive berries? either a vine, figs? so can no fountain both yield salt water and fresh." What he is talking about here is this: That when things are put together right, when they are natural, we bless God and we bless our fellow men. But sin and wrong and evil are unnatural. They are not according to God's infinite plan, and James illustrates that in nature. You do not see a fig tree bearing olives. And you do not see a grape vine bearing figs. It is not natural. It is against what God had intended and what God has made. So it is, James says, when a man's words and his tongue are used to hurt and to injure. It is not natural. It is not what God intended. It is not what God made. For with my tongue and with my mouth I am to bless. It is with my tongue and with my mouth that I pray, that I talk to God, that I tell Jesus about all the things in my deepest soul.

Recently I went to call on a man of God, one of the sweetest members of my church. He is in a rest home. His age is against him and his mind wanders. So as I sat down by him and we talked, he began to cry and said, "You know, I just get so lonely and I get so sad.

But then do you know what I do? I get down by the side of my bed and I tell Jesus all about it and, when I tell Jesus all about it, the burden is lifted from my heart and I'm not lonely, and I'm not sad anymore." What a sweet thing for a man to know, that he can kneel down and talk to Jesus and say words to the blessed Savior. Is it right, that with the same tongue, the same voice, and the same words by which I take my soul to Jesus, I should use that tongue to lash out or to bear a tale that brings agony to someone else. It is not right. James says these things ought not so to be. With the tongue we bless God; it is with our mouth that confession is made unto salvation. Romans 10:9, 10 says, "If thou shalt confess with thy mouth the Lord Jesus, and shalt believe in thine heart that God hath raised him from the dead, thou shalt be saved. For with the heart man believeth unto righteousness; and with the mouth confession is made unto salvation." It is with our tongues that we confess our Savior openly. It is with our mouths that we witness to the saving grace of our Lord. In Revelation 12 we read "And they overcame him (our great adversary Satan) by the blood of the Lamb, and by the word of their testimony" (v.11). When we walk through the days of our lives we ought always to say a good word for Jesus. Someone in the store, someone coming down the street, someone who works in the office — always a good word for Jesus.

And when we say a good word for Jesus we receive the power of God to overwhelm and to overcome the powers of darkness. It would be impossible for me to say a good word for Jesus and at the same time use words that hurt, hinder, and cause anger, agony, and suffering. My words are to be in keeping with the Spirit of our Lord who tells us that when we are reviled, we revile not again. He tells us to pray for those who hurt us and despitefully use us. Always the Christian is to be meek in his response, no matter what or where.

With our tongues we confess unto salvation, and with our tongues we witness to the saving grace of Christ, and with our tongues we magnify the Lord. Magnify the Lord with me; praise the Lord with me. I do it in the words that I say, with the glory that I feel in my soul when I speak in syllables. This is the meaning of the last verse of Psalm 19, "Let the words of my mouth and the meditation of my heart, be acceptable in thy sight, O Lord, my strength, and my redeemer."

Chapter 9

OUR WORDS
(James 3:1-12)

In this chapter I would like to continue our discussion on James 3 about the "untamed tongue." In James 3:9 the pastor of the church in Jerusalem writes that with the tongue "bless we God, even the Father; and therewith curse we men, which are made after the similitude of God. Out of the same mouth proceedeth blessing and cursing. My brethren, these things ought not so to be. Doth a fountain send forth at the same place sweet water and bitter? . . . Who is a wise man and endued with knowledge among you? Let him shew out of a good conversation his works with meekness of wisdom."

God's Words

The words that we speak are all important, but we cannot emphasize too much the words of God. Matthew 4:4 avows, "Man shall not live by bread alone, but by every word that proceedeth out of the mouth of God." My favorite text, Isaiah 40:8, declares "The grass withereth, the flower fadeth, but the word of our God shall stand for ever." In Revelation 19:11-13, we read, "And I saw heaven opened, and behold a white horse; and he that sat upon him was called Faithful and True, and in righteousness he doth judge and make war. His eyes were as a flame of fire, and on his head were many crowns . . . he was clothed with a vesture dipped in blood: and his name is called The Word of God." John begins his Gospel with that avowal, "In the beginning was the Word, and the Word was with God, and the Word was God." It would be impossible for one to emphasize too much the Word of God.

Our Words

By the word of the Lord the heavens were created — the very stars were flung into their celestial orbit. By the word of God all that we see came into existence. By the word of God the universe is upheld. Hebrews 1:3 says, "upholding all things by the word of his power." By the word of God we are convicted, by the word of God we are saved. By the word of God we have assurance of our ultimate home in heaven. We cannot emphasize too much the word of God. It is identified with the Lord Himself. Both the spoken word and the incarnate Word are called the word of God.

Now that leads me to make a corollary emphasis. This is not just a deduction, an addendum, but it is the text of the Bible itself. It is God's revelation of Himself so the words are thus important.

Our Words

Our words also are important. For example, we are saved, we are born again by the words of our confession and of our faith. That is plainly stated in Romans 10:9 and 10, "If thou shalt confess with thy mouth the Lord Jesus, and shalt believe in thine heart that God hath raised him from the dead, thou shalt be saved. For with the heart man believeth unto righteousness (the kind that saves us); and with the mouth confession is made unto salvation." In Matthew 10:32 and 33 our Lord Himself taught us saying, "Whosoever therefore shall confess me before men, him will I confess also before my Father which is in heaven. But whosoever shall deny me before men, him will I also deny before my Father which is in heaven."

The unpardonable sin is something of the word, of language, of saying. "Whosoever speaketh against the Holy Ghost, it shall not be forgiven him, in this world, neither in the world to come" (Matt. 12:32). It is a remarkable thing we find in the Word of God when the Lord teaches us in Matthew 12 that we are to be judged in the final days by our words. He says in Matthew 12:34 and 35, "Out of the abundance of the heart the mouth speaketh. A good man out of the good treasure of the heart bringeth forth good things: and an evil man out of the evil treasure bringeth forth evil things."

You listen to a man talk and you will know exactly what he is on the inside. If he is filthy on the inside you will see it in his dirty language. If he is holy and pure on the inside you will see it in his chaste and beautiful language. "I say unto you, that every idle word that men shall speak, they shall give account thereof in the day of judgment." Now listen to this verse, "For by thy words thou shalt be justified, and by thy words thou shalt be condemned." It is not possible to emphasize too much the Word of God and the corollary that follows immediately, nor is it possible to emphasize too much the significance of our words, our language.

Our Words to God

First, I want to mention words addressed to God, and I shall refer to them as prayers, praise, and personification — our words that we address to God. I did not quite realize until I began this study, how the Lord speaks of our words in prayers. For example in Mark 11, the Lord says, "Verily I say unto you, that whosoever shall say unto this mountain, Be thou removed, and be thou cast into the sea; and shall not doubt in his heart, but shall believe that those things which he saith shall come to pass; he shall have whatsoever he saith." Words. Words spoken to the mountain will produce action.

Take again the words of our Lord in John 15, "If my words abide in you, ye shall ask what ye will, and it shall be done unto you." Our Lord defines our addressing God in prayer, as words, and those words brought with dedication, faith, and meaning, bring to pass what we ask. I did not say that, Jesus says that. Our words in prayer are significant and all-important. They are channels through which flows what is in our souls — the faith that lives within us.

Again, our praise to God is in words. "I will bless the Lord at all times," David sings in Psalm 34. "His praise shall continually be in my mouth. My soul shall make her boast in the Lord . . . . O magnify the Lord with me, and let us exalt His name together." It is in our words that we exalt our Lord and magnify His marvelous name.

We are to personify, to incarnate God's words. They are to be a part of us, what we are. If someone were to analyze us that's what he would find in us — the Word of God. If he were to take a graph of our heart he would find in us the Word of God. Listen to Paul as he writes in Colossians 3:16, "Let the word of Christ dwell in you richly in all wisdom; teaching and admonishing one another." Or listen to Simon Peter as he writes in 1 Peter 4:11, "If any man speak, let him speak the oracles of God (the words of God)."

Well, you say, how is it possible that a man can achieve a language like that? Let me tell you, and I do not exaggerate. I have heard many people, especially old-timers, who read the King James Version of the Bible day and night, and I have listened to those godly people speak. I am speaking mostly now of the days when I was a teenager and a pastor out in the country. Those people loved God's Book and they read it. It was about all that they read and certainly all they studied. Did you know that in their language they sounded like the Bible? I have heard those saintly people pray, and from the beginning of the petition to the end it was none other than the Word of God. It is remarkable how the Word of God can live in man's heart and how his language can reflect that holy and pure revelation of God. That is what we are commanded to do. In our speech we are commanded to reflect the incarnation of God's Word, God's peace, God's language in our souls.

OUR WORDS TO SATAN

Now the second part of our discussion concerns our words to Satan. I have just spoken of our words to God. The Lord in His Book speaks of our words to Satan. Listen to Revelation 12:11, "And they overcame him (and just above in the verse that 'him' is identified as that old serpent, the dragon, and Satan the devil) by the blood of the Lamb, and by the word of their testimony." They overcame him, *nichaio. Nichaio, nichaio,* they really pulverized him! It was a tremendous triumph. That is, it was not just barely a victory. They overcame him, they pulverized him, and they conquered him. They defeated him by the blood of the Lamb and by the word of their testimony, confronting and confounding Satan with words of commitment and devotion to Christ.

You know I got to thinking about that. I never saw it happen and I do not know that I ever did it myself, but I got to turning that over in my mind, the power of a man's testimony to pulverize Satan, absolutely to destroy him. And it is done by just man's testimony.

Let us look at that. Suppose there are three fellows in a locker room at the "Y" with you and one of them begins to tell a filthy story. Suppose I put my hand on the shoulder of one of the men and I put my other hand on the shoulder of the other and say, "Fellows, let's bow in prayer." I'll tell you that would be a new atmosphere.

Suppose a country boy goes to one of the big cities for the first time. He is walking down the street and he passes in front of a bawdy house where a female tries to entice him inside of that house, and the fellow says he would be happy to go in. So he goes in and he says, "You know what, I want to tell you about my conversion and how I found the Lord." I'll tell you there would be some surprised women in that place. I am just taking some examples to show you how a testimony for Jesus absolutely destroys the power of Satan.

Any time you find yourself in any trial or any temptation or in any enticement, just say a good word about Jesus. Just begin to testify for the Lord and see if the very angels of heaven do not surround you, bear you up on their wings in strength and in *nichaio*. Satan is no match for the Word of God and for the testimony of Jesus Christ. "And they overcame him by the blood of the Lamb, and by the word of their testimony."

We are to be absolutely unafraid of Satan. You may ask, How, in a world of disease, disaster, and death, how is it that we do not cringe at him? God teaches us to be unafraid. In the name of the Lord rebuke him. The Lord tells us in Luke 12 that when we fall into trials in the world we are not to let it be a burden to us, "For the Holy Ghost shall teach you in the same hour what ye ought to say." Do not be afraid of any situation that could develop, God will put His words in your mouth.

Our Words Concerning Ourselves

I speak now of our words concerning ourselves. I have spoken of our words addressed to God — praise, prayer, and personification incarnate in us. I have spoken of our words of testimony addressed to Satan that absolutely destroy him. I want to speak now of the words as they affect us. You know, when I study the Bible the things that I read are sometimes overwhelming. I can hardly realize them. In our text James writes that our words, our tongues, can defile the whole body, make us dirty. The mouth is the open door to the soul and when our mouth is filthy the whole sewer pours in and the whole physical frame is defiled. When you talk filthy you get filthy. Your language somehow interferes into every fiber of your being and you get unclean just like the language you use. If one is dirty, the other is dirty.

Let us turn that around. It would mean also that pure and chaste language brings health and life and cleansing to the body. Listen to these words from Proverbs 4. "My son, attend to my words; incline thine ear unto my sayings. Let them not depart from thine eyes; keep them in the midst of thine heart. For they are life unto those that find them, and health to their flesh."

I do not invent these things. I repeat, I am just an echo, I am just a voice. I read these things in God's Book. If a man will use beautiful, kind, clean, chaste, pure language God says it will bring life to him and health to his flesh. You know that doctors sometimes use the word psychosomatic. *Psyche* is the Greek word for mind. *Soma* is the Greek word for body. Anything somatic is of the body, so psychosomatic refers to the influence of the mind over the body. That is a word you will find the doctor using often as he looks at his patient. Psychosomatic ailments and troubles indicate that there is nothing wrong with a person's heart or his stomach, or anything else, but he is under a tremendous mental or emotional problem and his body reflects it. They call that a psychosomatic ailment. Now that is exactly what the Bible is saying. A long time before men of medicine began writing their tomes and teaching in medical schools, God wrote it here. How I speak out of my soul has a great repercussion in my physical frame. And if I am vile and unclean it has an effect in my body. But if I am clean and pure in my words and my language, it brings health to those who thus speak and thus think. Is that not a remarkable thing? And all of this comes out of God's Word.

Our Words Concerning Others

Having written of our words addressed to God, and our words addressed to Satan, and our words in their effect upon ourselves, we mention now our words as they concern others. How am I to speak to others. This is what I am not to say. I am not to be a backbiter or a whisperer. I want you to look at the company in which the apostle Paul by divine inspiration puts backbiters, whisperers, defamers, and slanderers. I am going to read the closing verses of Romans 1, talking about those corrupt people of the Greco-Roman world in which Paul lives. He speaks of the fact that they did not retain God in their knowledge and therefore God gave them over to a reprobate mind. Their minds were filled with all unrighteousness. Look at these words, "fornication, wickedness, covetousness, maliciousness; full of envy, murder, debate, deceit, malignity; whisperers, backbiters, haters of God, despiteful, proud, boasters, inventors of evil things, disobedient to parents, without understanding, covenant-breakers, without natural affection, implacable, unmerciful: Who knowing the judgment of God, that they which commit such things are worthy of death."

Imagine that — the murderer, the fornicator, the covenant-breaker, the implacable, and unmerciful, the inventors of evil and the disobedient. The whisperer, the defamer, and the slanderer are classed in the same breath with the murderer, the fornicator, the implacable, and the disobedient. What our words can do for us!

The Book of Leviticus may appear difficult to read, but listen to Leviticus 19:16, "Thou shalt not go up and down as a talebearer among the people." That is what we are not to do. Listen to the wisest man who ever lived as he tells us in Proverbs 11:13, "A talebearer revealeth secrets: but he that is of a faithful spirit concealeth the matter." Listen again as he writes in Proverbs 18:8: "The words of a talebearer are as wounds, and they go down into the innermost parts of the belly." They plunge into the very soul of a man. Listen to Proverbs 26:20, "Where no word is, there the fire goeth out: so where there is no talebearer, the strife ceaseth." All you have to do, God says, to have peace and quiet among God's people, is just do not whisper, do not bear tales, do not slander and defame, do not repeat what you hear. Keep it to yourself and God.

If I am not to be a talebearer and a whisperer and a defamer and a slanderer then what am I to do? This is what I am to do. I am to speak beautifully, graciously, and kindly. The apostle Paul writes, "Speak every man truth with his neighbour: for we are members one of another. . . . Let no corrupt communication proceed out of your mouth, but that which is good to the use of edifying, that it may minister grace unto the hearers."

There is always something good we can say. When you say it make it good. If we do that with our mouths and our words we magnify God, we testify to the grace of the Lord Christ Jesus and we seek to encourage each other. You will find a new life and a new happiness.

Chapter 10

GETTING THINGS FROM GOD
(James 4:1-3)

We now come to the fourth chapter of James where we will look at the first three verses. "From whence come wars and fightings among you? come they not hence, even of your lusts that war in your members? Ye lust, and have not: ye kill, and desire to have, and cannot obtain: ye fight and war, yet ye have not, because ye ask not. Ye ask, and receive not, because ye ask amiss, that ye may consume it upon your lusts."

There are some words in the passage that in 1611 might have reflected the true meaning that James meant, but to us they have a somewhat different color and connotation. He says, "Do not these troubles that arise between you arise of your lusts that war in your members?" The word is *hedonai*; common words in the English language are "hedonism," "hedonistic," that is, "pleasure-loving." Lust has a different meaning today, but *hedonai* means "self-gratification," "ministering to oneself," "pleasure." In the second verse the words "ye lust and have not," *epithumia*, does not mean "lust" as we think of it. It means "to long for earnestly," "to desire." Then James says we ask and receive not because we ask amiss. *Kakos* literally means "badly," can mean "evilly." *Dapanao* means to "spend wastefully, luxuriously" — "that ye may consume it upon your lusts." There again the word is *hedonai*, for selfish pleasure.

So James is writing about why we do not get things from God. He speaks of prayer not in the sense of communion or fellowship or a surrendered yieldedness to God, but as an instrument, a means of receiving things from the hand of God. How do you do that?

75

Try to Pray

First of all, let me say that most people do not even try to pray. Prayer is extraneous to their thoughts and to their lives. To the natural man prayer would be a burdensome task. Paul wrote in 1 Corinthians 2:14, "But the natural man receiveth not the things of the Spirit of God: for they are foolishness unto him: neither can he know them, because they are spiritually discerned." The same inspired apostle Paul wrote in Romans 8:7, "The carnal mind is enmity against God: for it is not subject to the law of God, neither indeed can be." And he said further that "the flesh cannot please God." So to an unspiritual man, to a natural man, the man of the flesh, the carnal man, prayer is extraneous and is looked upon as a burden and a tedious task.

Even in our churches you will find that same holdover from our old carnal nature. To many, prayer would be a wearisome assignment. I can see that in how people respond to an invitation to come to dinner, an invitation for entertainment — they will be there. But when they are invited to pray, they find other places that to them are more alluring and attractive. And of course to a skeptic, an unbeliever, prayer is absolutely impertinent. It has no meaning whatsoever. Prayer is nothing to an unbelieving world.

Frustrations in Prayer

Now when we come to ourselves, we who are Christians, and have been baptized into the faith and belong to the household of God, we also find frustration in prayer for we ask and we do not receive. That seems such a diametrical contradiction to what our Lord wrote. You read Luke's account of it in his 11th chapter. Matthew makes it a part of the Sermon on the Mount, and our Lord said in Matthew 7:7, "Ask, and it shall be given you; seek, and ye shall find; knock, and it shall be opened unto you. For every one that asketh receiveth; and he that seeketh findeth; and to him that knocketh it shall be opened." Then he added, "If ye then, being evil, know how to give good gifts to your children, how much more shall your Father which is in heaven give good things to them that ask him?"

So we ask and we get nothing. That is why the apostle writes this passage. We do not have because we do not ask. And we ask and

Getting Things From God 77

receive not because we ask *kakos,* we do not ask correctly. God has put this world together in such a way that it runs according to certain principles and certain laws. If we obey those principles and those laws we find a response, a return; but if we do not, we do not find a response and we do not find a return. It has to be done according to the way God set it up, and to tell whether or not we are obeying the law, being obedient to the principle of God. If we have a problem in mathematics, the answer to whether or not we did it right is the sum of it. Is it correct? If we had a machine, the answer to whether the thing is put together right or not is whether it does what we want it to do. Does it run and does it produce?

So it is in the matter of prayer — of getting things from God. If we do it right we have to use the instrument in a correct way. If we get what we want, we have to do it in the way God set it up. No matter what kind of an instrument or how effectively it may be put together, if it is not used correctly, then it will not work right. For example, when our little fellow Cris was a baby he was in a high chair eating at the table. He had a spoon in his hand and he was trying to eat with the spoon turned upside down. Did you ever try to eat with a spoon turned upside down? It is the opposite of what you want. It does not scoop up. You have to turn it up to make it scoop up. So I took his little hand and turned the spoon up, but, sure enough, he turned it backside up again and tried to eat, cramming it into his mouth. The spoon was made to be used one way, and any other way does not work.

Principles of Praying

Now all the things in God's universe are like that. He put it together in a certain way and when we follow that way and follow those principles and those laws, it works beautifully. But when we do not do it that way, when we do not follow the principles and the laws of the Lord, then we follow into ways that lead to frustration and defeat and sometimes abject despair. So the apostle, writing here about prayer, says: (1) we do not have simply because we do not ask; and (2) when we do ask, we do not receive because we ask badly that we may consume it wastefully, spending it on our own personal pleasures. All of us are made pretty much alike and apparently there is no limit to our wanting. If we have two cars, we want a third one. If we have one, we want a second one. If we are affluent enough to have a beautiful townhouse, we would like to have one also out in the country. If we have a million dollars, we want two. If we have 500 million dollars, we want a billion. The people who are the most avaricious and grasping for money are rich people. There seems to be no satiation to the wants of some people. They just expand and expand, and the more they have, the more they want. Nations also are like that. This is why the apostle writes about wars and fighting and where they come from. It is because the things people seek and desire and covet, they want more and more of. So nations come to bitter grips about possessions.

Today we have an oil problem. Someday we are going to find that when it comes to a choice between the poverty and impoverishment of industrialized nations and seizing the oil, I can tell you what will happen. We will attempt to seize the oil. That is the way humanity is. We are just made that way. So James says that in our praying, we do not get much of what we ask for because we use God. Why should there be a God, we say to ourselves, if He cannot be used? So we use Him and we ask in order that we may consume what we ask for on our own selfish pleasures.

Unanswered Prayer

The Scriptures reveal to us many reasons why we ask and do not receive. For one thing, we do not expect it. We ask without any expectation of our prayer being answered. The Lord told a man one time that according to his faith, would it be done to him. Sometimes we ask indifferently. We do not agonize. The Lord spoke of that when He spoke of our importunity in prayer — to pray, to ask, to ask again and again. Sometimes we do not get our answer because we have harshness in our hearts toward others. The Lord said that when we pray, if we have anything against our brother, we are to forgive him, and ask him to forgive us. Then sometimes our prayers are not answered because of sin in us. The psalmist said if we regard iniquity in our hearts, the Lord will not hear us. Isaiah 59:1,2 says, "Behold, the LORD's hand is not shortened, that it cannot save; neither his ear heavy, that it cannot hear: But your iniquities have separated between you and your God, and your sins have hid his face from you, that he will not hear." So these things interfere. They come between us and God.

But He also says, and this is the emphasis of this chapter, that there are times when we have not because we ask not. We just don't take it to God in prayer.

> I got up early one morning and rushed right into the day.
> I had so much to accomplish that I didn't have time to pray.
> Problems just tumbled about me and each task seemed heavier.
> Why doesn't God help me? I wondered,
> And God answered, "You didn't ask."
> I tried to come into God's presence and use all my keys at the lock.
> God gently and lovingly chided me, "My child, you didn't knock."
> I wanted to see joy and beauty but the day wore on gray and bleak.
> I wondered why God didn't show me, but I didn't seek.
> So I woke up early this morning and paused before entering the day.
> I had so much to accomplish that I had to take time to pray.

The reason we do not have help from heaven is we do not ask for it. We do not take it to God. We do not make it a matter of prayer. We rush into the day ourselves, make decisions for ourselves and leave God out of it. Then we wonder why life can be so frustrating and disappointing. You know, it is a marvelous thing how God can be moved to answer if we just ask Him. I stumbled into this thought in Psalm 107. The psalmist talks about a man who is sick unto death and in his extremity he prays. Then he talks about a mariner, a sailor in a storm, and in the agony and terror of the hurricane and a boat about to sink, the man prays. And in both instances the man is heard. God heard him and saved him. But the psalmist wonders why we do not take our needs to God in our extremities. Listen to the psalmist. "Their soul abhorreth all manner of meat; and they draw near unto the gates of death. Then they cry unto the LORD in their trouble, and he saveth them out of their distresses. He sent his word, and healed them, and delivered them from their destructions. Oh that men would praise the LORD for his goodness, and for his wonderful works to the children of men!" (vv. 18-21). Now he is going to talk about the mariner. "They that go down to the sea in ships, that do business in great waters; These see the works of the Lord, and his wonders in the deep. For he commandeth, and raiseth the stormy wind, which lifteth up the waves thereof. They mount up to the heaven, they go down again to the depths: their soul is melted because of trouble. They reel to and fro, and stagger like a drunken man, and are at their wit's end. Then they cry unto the Lord in their trouble, and he bringeth them out of their distresses. He maketh the storm a calm, so that the waves thereof are still. Then are they glad because they be quiet; so he bringeth them unto their desired haven. Oh that men would praise the LORD for his goodness, and for his wonderful works to the children of men!" (vv. 23-31). God answers prayer. He just does. A sick man does not pray, but in his final, agonizing moment he asks God and God hears him. Here are sailors who never think about God or, if they do, they use His name in vain like many of our politicians. Is that not tragic? How can God bless America when our men in highest office use God's name in vain? Many are like drunken sailors who get into deep trouble and finally call on the name of the Lord — and He hears them. He's that kind of a God. We do not have because we do not ask. We do not make it a matter of prayer.

ANSWERED PRAYER

Recently I came across the story of a sweet little boy. He was a German lad and was so devout — he loved the Lord and he prayed often. His father and mother were very dilatory, but the little boy was devout. The pastor would speak of him in praise for his godliness and holiness. The headmaster of the school had told the children to be sure they were always on time. So the little boy sought to be on time when he went to school. One morning, on account of his parents, the little boy could not get away, and when he walked out the door to go to school, the clock struck the time that he was to be there. It was a long walk from his house to the schoolhouse and the little fellow bowed his head and prayed aloud, "Oh, Lord, don't let me be late for school." A man nearby overheard the boy's prayer and he thought it unthinkable. It had already struck time for the boy to be there, yet he prayed God would not let him be late for school. And out of curiosity the man followed the boy just to see what would happen. You know what happened? The headmaster of the school had put his key in the lock and somehow had turned it the wrong way, and he jammed the lock. He could not get the door open. They called for a locksmith, the locksmith had finished his work, and the door opened and the headmaster and the students walked in just as that devout little boy arrived! Isn't that blessed? Ask, He says. Make it a matter of prayer. Ask.

Ask and Receive

"Ask, and ye shall receive." Jesus does not say we have to study a book about it. We do not have to be learned. We do not have to have a doctor's degree. We do not have to have a diploma in theology. Just as we talk to our own father, so the Lord invites us to talk to Him. The high and mighty, the low and menial, all of us — just ask. Sometimes God will say it is not best. When Moses pled with the Lord to let him go over into the Promised Land, God told him to speak no more of the matter. The answer was no. When the Lord prayed, "Father, let this cup pass from me," God said no. And the Lord died on the cross. When Paul asked the Lord to remove his thorn in the flesh, God said, "No, My strength is made perfect in weakness; My grace is sufficient for you." God may say no, but God's rule and God's principle is that we ask. That is the way He has put it together. It pleases God that we ask. In Psalm 2:8 we read, "Ask of me, and I shall give thee the heathen for thine inheritance, and the uttermost parts of the earth for thy possession." But it says, "Ask." Even the Lord Jesus was to pray. It was the purpose of God to bless all Israel, but Samuel had to pray for the blessing. It was the purpose of God in the days of Elijah to send the rain, but Elijah had to pray for it. When Daniel read in the prophet Jeremiah that after seventy years God was to visit His people and they could return home, Daniel still had to pray for it. It was the purpose of God to save the Gentiles and He raised up Paul to preach the gospel to the Gentiles, but he had to pray for us that we might be saved. That is the way God has put it together.

Why does not God just do it anyway — without our asking? I do not know. I just know that the principle and rule and program of God is that I ask Him. That is the way God makes it work. No stewardship program in any church will ever succeed if the people involved do not pray. Children will not grow up to pray if parents do not pray for them and teach them to pray. So it is with the spirit of our churches. If we would feel God's presence, we must ask Him in saving grace to walk among us, to sit by our side, to live in our hearts.

> Come Holy Spirit, heavenly Dove,
> With all Thy quickening powers;
> Kindle a flame of sacred love
> In these cold hearts of ours.

We cannot do this without prayer. Unless a people pray and ask God for guidance, they will be thrown into wars and conflicts. If we do pray, God will give us above all that we ask or think. The apostle Paul closed his prayer in Ephesians 3 with these words, "Now unto him who is able to do exceeding abundantly above all that we ask or think, according to the power that worketh in us, Unto him be glory in the church by Christ Jesus throughout all ages, world without end. Amen." "Above all that we ask or think" — if you ask, God will do above all that you ask for and all that you could even think of: Abraham asked God for Ishmael. The Lord was pleased and said, "I'll make of Ishmael a great people" — all those Arab people. But He gave Abraham more than he asked for. When he was one hundred years old and when Sarah was ninety years old, God gave them Isaac. Above all that we ask or think. Jacob said, "Lord, if You'll just give me raiment and food and bring me back home, I'll give the tenth to You." When God brought him back to Bethel, Jacob was enriched immeasureably. Solomon said, "Lord, give me wisdom," and God gave him everything else besides. When the transgressor, the thief on the other side of the Lord Jesus prayed, "Lord, remember me," Jesus said to him, "Today, this day, you'll be with Me in paradise." When the prodigal son came back to his father saying, "Father, I'm not worthy to be called your son. Just make me one of these menial hired servants, send me out in the field and just give me the wages of a hired hand," the father said, "Bring the finest robe and put it on him, and put a ring upon his finger, and kill the fatted calf, for this my boy is dead and is alive again, he was lost and is found." And they began to rejoice. Above all that we ask or think. Ask Him. Make it a matter of prayer. "Lord, I don't know the decision to make in this." Ask Him. James says, "If any of you lack wisdom, let him ask of God, that giveth to all men liberally." "Lord, I have a problem in my life." Take it to God. "Lord, I've got troubles or I have needs." Take it to the Lord. He will answer. You will have a new life and a new hope and a new uplift in your soul. There will be a heavenwardness, a Christwardness in you that you never knew before if you will just ask.

Chapter 11

THE QUALITY
(James 4:13-16)

As we continue our study of James 4, we turn to verse 13: "Go to now, ye that say, Today or Tomorrow we will go into such a city, and continue there a year, and buy and sell, and get gain: Whereas ye know not what shall be on the morrow. For what is your life? It is even a vapour, that appeareth for a little time, and then vanisheth away. For that ye ought to say, If the Lord will, we shall live, and do this, or that. But now ye rejoice in your boastings: all such rejoicing is evil." The pastor avows an axiomatic truth to all of us. God gives us memories to reflect on the past, but He has not given us eyes to discern the future. No man knows what any tomorrow may bring. There must have been a kindness and a goodness of God in thus veiling the future from our eyes, for if a man knew what the morrow would bring, he would live in constant fear and foreboding. Dying, he would die a thousand deaths before dying just once. Fainting, he would faint a thousand times under a stroke that was yet to be delivered. God hides the future from our eyes that we might live in confidence and in hope. And that is why the pastor of the church in Jerusalem, our Lord's brother, writes whereas we do not know what shall be on the morrow, therefore we ought to say, "If God wills, I will do this and that." But the man who looks upon himself as all-sufficient and all-adequate, he is the man who says this year I am going to do thus and so, and next year I am going to do thus and so and five years and maybe ten and twenty years from now I will add estates to my possessions. Thus the man lives in boastful, prideful self-assurance and self-confidence. "But now ye rejoice in your boastings." The word *kaukasthe* actually means "to boast." "But now ye rejoice — you are boasting in your show" (*alazonea*, which means "show"). He boasts in his supposed superiority, his ostentatious self-confidence. He knows what he is going to do. He knows what he is going to be. He knows what the morrow brings and, without God, and without even feeling the need of the blessings of the Lord, he lives his life in prideful self-assurance.

What Is Life?

The pastor, addressing himself to that, says that a man is not right when he lives that way and when he purposes to live a life as though it were mortgaged to him. But James says that a man ought to say, "If God will help me and if the Lord will stand by me and if God gives me breath and length of days, I shall do this and that in His will." Now, the ultimate reason for what he says is in the text. "For what is your life? It is even a vapour, that appeareth for a little time, and then vanisheth away." Now that is an interesting question he raises. What is your life? Some answers are given in earth's best literature; for example Hans Christian Anderson wrote, "Life is a fairy tale, written by God's finger." Robert Browning wrote, "Life is probation and the earth is not the goal, but the starting point." Thomas Carlysle wrote, "Life is a little gleam of time between two eternities." Goethe wrote, "Life is the childhood of our immortality." William Shakespeare wrote, "Life is a tale told by an idiot, full of sound and fury, signifying nothing." Henry Thoreau wrote, "Life is like a stroll upon the beach."

To us who love the Lord and have given our hearts to Him, it is interesting to read in the Scriptures what God says about life. Job said our life is like the "sparks that fly upward." He says it is like a messenger sent swiftly on his way. It is like a ship crossing the bosom of the sea. Job said life is like an eagle darting to its prey, so swiftly done. In Isaiah 40, the inspired prime minister of Judah said life is like a flower that fades and like the grass that withers. And in our text, the pastor of the church in Jerusalem wrote, "What is your life? It is even a vapour, that appeareth for a little time and then vanisheth away." There is an insubstantiality in life that is undeniable. It is like our breath on a cold, frosty morning and how quickly it dissipates. It is like a brittle thread, not 1/10th of a substance of a spider's thread, so easily broken and torn apart. And our text tells us how quickly it

The Quality

vanishes away. Our life soon is shattered like Nero's golden palace. It is gone like the hanging gardens of Babylon. It is destroyed like the beautiful pillars of the seventh wonder of the world, the Ephesian temple of Diana. It is lost in the innumerable rows of graves in a cemetery. Forgotten. However you garnish a tomb, the most common thing that I know is a grave.

How soon life vanishes away. There are certainties about life and number one is that it is ending. Its certain and inevitable conclusion is that we die — sometimes so suddenly, so tragically. We cast ourselves upon the mercies of God that God will give us breath and length of days. Death can come so quickly, so suddenly, without announcement, without any foreboding — just suddenly sweep us away. It is like the grass before the oncoming reaping of the scythe, like a leaf that falls from an autumnal branch. How soon our strength can be turned into weakness and our comeliness into destruction and corruption. The Lord by Isaiah sent word to Hezekiah the king telling him to set his house in order for he would die. Who can spare us and save us from that judgment? It is inevitable. A man in the service of his country is not protected from death, even by his patriotism. A child surrounded by love and affection is not shielded from that grim reaper. And a man in his affluence and in his abundance cannot buy one other breath of life if God says the time has come. All of us alike belong to an army, engaged in a war from whence there is no discharge. We march in ranks on a field, subject to the darts of death, with no protection for breast or back. Like a stream carrying us to a great fall, we are borne, even in our sleep, on the breast of the river of life to its ultimate and final plunge.

What Is Death?

Now, what is to be our attitude toward death? I have said nothing strange or unusual. I have just repeated what all of us intuitively know and experientially see. What is our attitude toward that inevitable judgment? Well, for those of the world, I can understand why it would be a catastrophe and a midnight darkness. The man may boast in himself, but he cannot hide from his eyes the reality of death. Is that not a strange irony of fate, that a man can obviate the cross of Christ, but not death? He can push far from him the appeal of Christ, but not the grave. All of us stand at just a measured distance from its open tomb. And the man of the world, however strong and able and well, has a skeleton in his closet. It is death. He has a specter at the foot of his bed. It is death. And he has a cancer in all of his worldly plans and joys. It is death. But how different this all is to the man who bows in the presence of God and says, that if the Lord wills and if He gives him life, then he will do this or that. Death to that man is but a call from God to higher and holier things.

Peter Waldo founded the Waldensian church centuries ago. He was the scion of a wealthy, affluent family, and was living his life as so many young, affluent men do, in a big way. He was at a dinner party and the young friend seated by his side suddenly dropped his head to the table and died. It was a shock to young Peter Waldo, and he began to search for some answers to the meaning of life. And he found it in God. Thereafter Peter Waldo, giving up his life of ease and fortune, stood on the streets, in the marketplace, on the highway where men passed by, and preached the gospel of the grace of the Son of God. Martin Luther was a nominal Christian and churchman. One day, as a young man, he was walking side by side with a friend when lightning came from heaven and struck his friend, and he died before Martin Luther's eyes. After that the big German gave his life to a search for the meaning of God's breath in us. One of the noblemen of England, on his way to his execution, passed by his clergyman. He stopped, took out his watch, and placed it in the hands of the minister and said, "Sir, the timepiece is yours. I am now to live in eternity." Ah, these are knockings at the door. Every grave, every cemetery, every passing hour is an emissary from heaven. There is a day coming, an inevitable hour when God shall take our breath, and we shall stand open and naked before Him with whom we have to do.

What Is the Meaning of Life?

And that brings me to the heart of the chapter. What is the wisdom of God in teaching us the meaning of life? Listen to God's Word: "I am come that they might have life, and that they might have it more abundantly" (John 10:10). Is that not an amazing thing? Often a child of the world will say or think, "I don't want to be a Christian, nor do I want to give my life to God. For I want to have a good time and I want to live and I want to drink life's joys to the fullest." God says the opposite is true. "I am come that they might have life, and have it

The Quality

more aboundingly, overflowingly, abundantly." It was the Lord who said, "I am the way, the truth, and the life." It was the Lord who said in the presence of death, "I am the resurrection and the life."

What is that life? That kind of life? It is not found in the abundance of things. Our Lord told the rich man who pulled down his barns to build greater, because he was so affluent, that God would knock at his door and require his soul. And then who would own the full barns? For, said our Lord, a man's life consists not in the abundance of the things that he possesses. I can easily understand that if a man's life is stocks and bonds, or real estate and possessions, that death is a nightmare, a grim reaper, a king of terrors. I can understand that, for that is not life — it is a travesty on it.

Nor does a man's life consist in the length of days. Methuselah was 969 years old when he died. The Lord was 33. I know nothing about Methuselah except that he lived and died at 969 years. But, what our blessed Lord in 33 years means to us and to the world!

What is this life then that the Lord describes as being real living? It is this. It is when a man says he will live and do this and that in God's will. When the man builds his days around God, when in humble surrender he bows before the Lord, then he begins to live. Let me illustrate this. Remember the story of the prodigal son? He left his father's house, took his inheritance, and lived it up. The Bible says "in riotous living." He was wasting his life upon harlots. He was having what the world calls "a big time." But when the young man came to his sense and came back home, do you remember what his father said? "This my son was dead and is alive again. He was lost and is found." God called that death. Even the apostle Paul wrote that the woman who lives in pleasures is dead while she lives. It is life when a man is born in the faith unto God. The sainted apostle Paul wrote in Ephesians 2:1 that we who were dead in trespasses and in sin God has "quickened" to a new life in Christ. This is the life. John wrote, "He that hath the Son hath life." We are born into the resurrected glory of our Lord and upon us who have already died there is no other death, just victory, triumph, and translation. That which the world calls death is nothing but a biological change to the body — ashes to ashes, and dust to dust. But that is not death in the Bible. For us who love Jesus it is a sleeping in Him. The world never heard of the word "cemetery" until the Christians invented it as the place where they lay asleep their beloved dead — waiting the resurrection day of our Lord. To the Christian, what the world calls death is but a sounding of the trumpets on the other side of the river as one of God's chosen children comes home. What they call death, is to us nothing but the angels coming to take us up into Abraham's bosom. What they call death is nothing but the sailor coming home from the sea and the hunter from the hills. Robert Louis Stevenson wrote a little poem to be inscribed on his tomb and it is there to this day:

> Under the wide and starry sky,
> Dig the grave and let me lie.
> Glad did I live and gladly die
> And I laid me down with a will.
>
> This be the verse you gave for me:
> Here he lies where he longed to be;
> Home is the sailor, home from the sea,
> And the hunter home from the hill.

That is death to the child of God — coming into port, the pilgrim coming home. If for me to live is Christ, to die is a gain. If for me to live is the world, to die is a loss. If for me to live is money, to die is a loss. If for me to live is sinful pleasure, to die is a loss. If for me to live is self, to die is a loss. But if for me to live is Christ, to die is a gain. Oh, blessed hope, precious comfort.

CHAPTER 12

THE COMING OF THE LORD
(James 5:7-9)

James joins the rest of the New Testament writers in introducing the greatest of all subjects, the coming of the Lord. He says in James 5:7-9: "Be patient therefore, brethren, unto the coming [the *parousia*, the coming alongside, the presence] of the Lord. Behold, the husbandman [the farmer] waiteth for the precious fruit of the earth, and hath long patience for it, until he receive the early and latter rain. Be ye also patient; stablish your hearts: for the coming of the Lord draweth nigh. Grudge not one against another [do not have a volitive spirit toward each other] brethren, lest ye be condemned: behold, the judge standeth before the door." There are two thoughts in the text that we shall try, under God, to present. One will be our waiting in patience before the coming of the Lord. And the other is the Judge standing at the door at the coming of the Lord.

Recently, I read a book about the Apocalypse by a learned professor, and the thesis of his book is this: There is no prophecy in the Book of Revelation. It would be meaningless, he said, to those persecuted Christians in the Roman Empire who were groaning under the iron heel and nailed fist of the Caesar to tell them to be strengthened and comforted, for a thousand years from now this will come to pass and that will come to pass. So he took the Book of Revelation and made all of it apply to something that was happening then and there. His thesis was, I repeat, that it is no comfort to God's people to tell them that there is an event that will come to pass in the future. I wonder what the professor would think about my text, when the pastor of the church at Jerusalem, James, the Lord's brother, exhorts his people to be patient unto the coming of the Lord. It has already been almost 2,000 years since James wrote and He has not come yet. Is there comfort and strength in the promise of the imminency of the return of Jesus? The Bible tells us to live our lives in expectation of the soon return of our Savior. To us it may be a long time, but not to Him. He says that a thousand years with God are but as a day. That would mean, then, that our Lord has been gone about two days. Maybe the third day He will return. But in any event, the Scriptures are welded together by that bonding expectancy and hope that our lives are not lived in vain, that there is Someone, a great God and Savior who is soon coming — He is standing, even at the door. And in the light of that, we are encouraged to be patient and expectant, and to live in that blessed hope of our soon victorious redemption.

PATIENCE

I want us to look for a moment at that word patience. For example, Paul wrote in Philippians 4:5, "Let your [*epiecese*] be known unto all men. The Lord is at hand." *Epiecese* – what would that mean? It means literally, if I can use several words in English to put it together, a humble and bowed spirit, yieldedness and surrender in the presence of the Lord. It is not being ostentatious, proud, or lifted up. The life of the Christian is always to be one of gentle humility, of bowing in yielded surrender to the will and presence of the Lord. I think I could present that in a contrast I found in my study. There is a Christian, unknown to me, who has written a parody on the famous poem by William Hendley entitled "Invictus." *Invictus* is the Latin word for "unconquerable" or "invincible." Hendley writes:

> Out of the night that covers me,
> Black as the Pit from pole to pole,
> I thank whatever gods may be
> For my unconquerable soul.
>
> In the fell clutch of circumstance,
> I have not winced nor cried aloud;
> Under the bludgeonings of chance
> My head is bloody, but unbowed.
>
> Beyond this place of wrath and tears
> Looms but the horror of the shade;
> And yet the menace of the years
> Finds, and shall find, me unafraid.

> It matters not how strait the gate,
> How charged with punishments the scroll,
> I am the master of my fate;
> I am the captain of my soul.

There is hardly a young person who has not studied that in English and in American literature. This is the parody written by Dorothea Day, a humble Christian:

> Out of the light that dazzles me,
> Bright as the sun from pole to pole,
> I thank the God I know to be,
> For Christ the Conqueror of my soul.
>
> Since His the sway of circumstance,
> I would not wince nor cry aloud;
> Under that rule which men call chance,
> My head with joy is humbly bowed.
>
> Beyond this place of sin and tears
> That life with Him and His the aid,
> That, spite the menace of the years
> Keeps and shall keep me unafraid.
>
> I have no fear though strait the gate,
> He cleared from punishment the scroll;
> Christ is the Master of my fate,
> Christ is the Captain of my soul.

This is the spirit of the Christian life that your gentle yieldedness be seen before all men, for the Lord is at hand. This is the meaning of the patient waiting for the coming of our Christ.

The Harvest

And James uses an illustration. He speaks of the husbandman, the farmer, who waits for the early and the latter rain, plants the crops, and looks to God for the harvest. He plants the seed in expectancy. Some of you may have seen a recent picture on the front page of your daily newspaper. Our government had sent a great tonnage of wheat to starving India and the picture showed the wheat which was to be planted for a harvest. But the hungry hordes were tearing apart the bins, were seizing the golden seed, and were consuming it in their starvation. My heart went out to the hungry people, but at the same time I thought how tragic that instead of patiently waiting for the harvest when the seed was planted, they were seizing it and destroying it. This is what feeds our mortal frames — the seed is planted and a farmer looks to God to speak to the clouds, to send the rain. He waits for the seed to quicken and to germinate, and then cultivating, plowing, and waiting he expects the harvest. He lives in that expectancy. He prepares for it, and when it comes, he is filled with thankfulness to God who gave it. So our lives are to be lived before the Lord. Our home is not here, it is there. Our reward is not here, it is there. Our expectancy is not here, it is there. And we live in the light of the soon coming of our blessed Jesus. Our inheritance is not here, it is there — home is in heaven, to where Jesus will take us when He comes again. How tragic it is not to prepare for heaven. No expectancy, no preparation, no planting, cultivating, tilling, no looking up to the face of God. Just to die in the night and nothing of hope and heaven beyond. Such is not the case with the Christian. He lives his life looking up in expectancy, in faithfulness, waiting for the coming of the Lord.

The second thought from our text reminds us we are to be kind and gracious to one another, forgiving and loving, not grudging one another lest we be condemned, for the Judge is standing before the door. He is there now. So this brings us to the truth of the great judgment day for the child of God.

THE JUDGMENT ON SIN

There are several judgments that are mentioned in the Scriptures. One is the judgment upon sin. That took place at Calvary when Christ died for our sins according to the Scriptures. Whether a man is saved or not is not determined at the end of the age. That judgment is here. John wrote in John 3:18, "He that believeth on him is not condemned: but he that believeth not is condemned already, because he hath not believed in the name of the only begotten Son of God." I am either saved now or I am lost *now*. The judgment of our salvation, the forgiveness of our sins is *now*. I accept or I reject and I am judged thereon *now*.

THE JUDGMENT OF THE NATIONS

Another judgment in the Bible is called the judgment of the nations in Matthew 25. All the Gentile nations are gathered before the Lord as He is seated upon His glorious throne. There is a judgment mentioned in Ezekiel 20 on Israel. There is a judgment upon the wicked dead in Revelation 20 where we read of the great white throne and how from the face of Him the heavens and the earth flee. And the lost stand before Him to receive the deeds done in their day in the flesh. What a horrible day that will be.

THE CHRISTIAN JUDGMENT

And then there is another judgment. This is the Christian judgment. "Behold, the judge standeth before the door." That judgment takes place when the Lord takes us to Himself in rapture and we are caught up to meet Him in the air. This is the first great thing that will happen when the dead are raised and those who are living at the coming of the Lord are transformed, immortalized, glorified in a moment, in the twinkling of the eye, at the last trump. When all of God's people are gathered to the Savior, we are taken up with Him into glory and there the first order will be the judgment of the Christians. It is not a judgment as to whether we are saved or lost. That judgment is now. But as the wicked dead are judged at the great white throne according to their deeds, so the Christian is caught up and stands at what the Bible calls the *bema*, the judgment seat of Christ, and there we receive our reward from the hands of Jesus.

He says for example in the Apocalypse, "Behold, I come quickly; and my reward is with me, to give every man according as his work shall be." What we do is written down with the point of a diamond in the Lamb's Book of Life and these works we have done, these deeds we have sought to do, become our inheritance and our reward forever and ever. That is why the reward is not given you when you die. If the Lord tarries and we fall asleep in the earth, we do not receive our reward when we die, because we do not "die" when we die. Our lives live on and on, our influence lives on and on in our children, in the people who knew us, in the family, among friends, and it continues on and on as long as time lasts. Only God is able to unravel the skein and to ferret out the influence of our lives and give us the reward of what we have done at the consummation of the age.

How wonderful and how beautiful that the Christian can live in expectancy of what God will do for him in heaven. He may be poor here, but rich up there. He may be crippled or blind here, but be young and well up there. He may live in a hovel here, but will live in a mansion there. He may be unknown here, not a half a dozen people care whether he lives or dies, but up there he is known as God knows him. Oh, the wonder and blessedness of what God has in store for those who love Him. That is the way the Christian is to live, as under God, knowing that the judge stands at the door. Any moment, any day, any hour there is nothing between us and being taken away into heaven. When there are no more prophecies to be fulfilled, He will come unannounced, unheralded, in a moment, in the twinkling of an eye, and just that suddenly we will be in the presence of our Lord. The fullness of life is to live and to work in the expectancy that God will reward His people. We are not to do what we do for the praise of men, for honor, for elevation. No! We ought to do what we do for the love of Jesus and depend on Him to reward us. That is why our lives ought to be filled with good things and why we ought to redeem the time.

An Illustration

Recently Mr. Pat Zondervan of The Zondervan Corporation in Grand Rapids, Michigan, made his annual pilgrimage to our church in behalf of the Gideons. He made his appeal for the distribution of the Holy Scriptures, and in that appeal held up in his hand a little white New Testament. One of the things the Gideons do is distribute these little white New Testaments to all the nurses of America. He told how a Christian nurse happened to have that little white New Testament in the pocket of her uniform one day and the outline of it was seen by one of her patients who was a lost man. He thought it was a package of cigarettes. So, seeing it there in her pocket, he asked her what brand she used. She told him it was no brand, took it out, and held it up for him to see and explained that it was a little New Testament, the Word of God. She asked if she could read to him out of it. He gave her permission, and as time passed she read to him again and again. And under the influence of the Holy Spirit the man was wonderfully saved. He confessed his sins, asked God to forgive him, and received the Lord Jesus into his heart. As the days passed, this Christian nurse had a strange impulse to go see the man. So she went to his room, and as she stood looking at him, he sat up in bed. He seemed to be looking at someone standing at the foot of the bed. Then he raised his arms and cried, "My Lord and my God," fell back, and his spirit was translated to heaven. Hearing that story, I could not help but bless the name of God for the little book and for the Holy

The Coming of the Lord

Spirit who carried its convicting message to the heart of that lost man. And praise God that he turned and accepted Jesus and was saved. Oh, how wonderful!

But again I cannot help but think what a sadness when a person gives his life to evil and to the world, and can just offer his soul to Jesus. What a tragedy to spend our influence and our days serving mammon and bring just a shell, just chaff to the Lord. What a sadness to go empty-handed, nothing to lay at His blessed feet.

> Must I go, and empty-handed?
> Must I meet my Saviour so?
> Not one soul with which to greet Him:
> Must I empty-handed go?

How much better to bring to Jesus a life as well as a soul. Do you remember how old Jesus was when He said, "Wist ye not that I must be about my Father's business?" Did He say that on the cross? Did He say that during His Galilean or Judean ministries? Did He say it at the threshold of manhood? No! He said that when He was twelve years old. Our years must be spent in the service of the great God who made us. We must work while it is day. The night is coming when no man can work. While I have my mind and while I have my strength may God help me to bring my best to lay at His dear feet. Then some day, not for what I did but for what I intended to do, God will receive me and bless me in His presence.

CHAPTER 13

PATIENCE OF JOB
(James 5:7-11)

You have all heard of "the patience of Job." But James also speaks of patience. "Be patient therefore, brethren, unto the coming of the Lord. Behold, the husbandman waiteth for the precious fruit of the earth, and hath long patience for it, until he receive the early and latter rain. Be ye also patient; stablish your hearts: for the coming of the Lord draweth nigh. Grudge not one against another, brethren, lest ye be condemned: behold, the judge standeth before the door. Take, my brethren, the prophets, who have spoken in the name of the Lord, for an example of suffering affliction, and of patience. Behold, we count them happy which endure. Ye have heard of the patience of Job, and have seen the end of the Lord; that the Lord is very pitiful, and of tender mercy."

"Ye have heard of the patience of Job, and have seen the end of the Lord." Yes, we have. But even though we have heard, yet sometimes we are prone to forget and it is needful that our memories be refreshed. We have heard, now let us hear again, for the gift of faith comes by our hearing. The apostle Paul wrote in Romans 10:17, "Faith cometh by hearing, and hearing by the word of God." Faith is the eyes of the soul. No one ever had a golden tongue who first did not have a silver ear. You must hear if you are to see with the eyes of the mind and of the soul. We have heard, we shall listen again, and we shall see that the Lord is of tender mercy. The end of the Lord — *telos* — the consummation of His purpose. When the Lord has done His work, it always is beautiful. It is good and gracious. God never purposed an evil thing for any of His creation, and least of all for the crown of His glory — the soul in the life of a man. The end of the Lord always is good for us. When the Lord looked at the beautiful firmament and the virgin earth, and had finished His creation, He said it was very good.

ADMONITION

In our text James has a triplet of admonitions concerning our being patient — and we always need them. It is a part of human weakness to grow restive under the providences and under the hand of God. The apostle tells us in verse 7 to be patient unto the coming of the Lord. And he repeats it. "Be ye also patient; stablish your hearts: for the coming of the Lord draweth nigh." Then again in verse 10: "Take, my brethren, the prophets, who have spoken in the name of the Lord, for an example of suffering affliction, and of patience." The voice of the Holy Spirit in our hearts is patience, the voice of the Holy Scriptures written on the sacred page is patience, the voice of our heavenly Father is patience, and the voice of our Savior is patience. But the classic example of all mankind is the reference in our text. "Ye have heard of the patience of Job, and have seen the end of the Lord; that the Lord is very pitiful, and of tender mercy."

Job was a patriarch. He lived in the time of the patriarchs — in the times of Abraham, Isaac, and Jacob. There is no reference in the Book of Job to any event or to any fact beyond the Book of Genesis. There is no reference to the law of Moses. There is no reference to the institutions of the Jews. The only references from events recorded in the Book of Genesis are to the Creation, to Adam, and to the Flood. This man Job was greatly tried. He lost everything he had — and he was a wealthy man. He lost all of his ten children — seven sons and three daughters. And he himself was grievously afflicted physically. We can look upon the affliction and suffering of others with nonchalance or disassociation, but when it comes to our bones and our flesh, it is something else. Job was covered with boils and sores from the crown of his head to the soles of his feet. He sat in an ash heap on a dung hill in misery and in agony. Every part of his body hurt and every nerve was a road on which armies of pain marched. To add to that was his own anguish of mind. His wife, who should have sustained him, prayed for him, encouraged him, and caused him to look up to heaven, told him to curse God and commit suicide. Curse God and die. What a wife!

To add to his anguish of mind, three "comforters" came to see Job, and were they not classics of assurance and encouragement! Job's three friends came to him and told him he must surely be a vile sinner, for only a vile sinner would suffer like that. They rubbed salt into his wounds. They threw dust into his eyes. They crowned his misery with suffering and agitation. The trials of Job were not imaginary. They were real. He was no hypochondriac. He was no hysterical groaner over imagined evils and hurts. He did not lose one child — he lost all ten of them. He did not lose a few hundred dollars — he lost his entire fortune. He was not just somewhat sick for an hour or a day — he was grievously afflicted and sat in pain and suffering and indescribable misery.

Why Do the Righteous Suffer?

Now how do we account for that? How is it that a good man suffers? The psalmist wanted to know the answer, too, as we see in Psalm 73. "As for me my feet were almost gone; my steps had well nigh slipped. For I was envious at the foolish, when I saw the prosperity of the wicked. . . . They are not in trouble as other men; neither are they plagued like other men. . . . Behold, these are the ungodly, who prosper in the world; they increase in riches. . . . For all the day long have I been plagued, and chastened every morning. . . . When I thought to know this, it was too painful for me; until I went into the sanctuary of God; then I understood." The closer a man gets to God, the more he understands the providences of God in the afflictions of the righteous. That is why we come to God's house to worship. In worship the minister explains to us from God's Word the ways of the Lord.

Maybe you feel this does not apply to you. You have not been introduced to such providences as that. Maybe not now, but you will be. There is no one who will escape, not one. When we were born into this world we were born into a world of trouble and some day we shall all suffer from it. Do you remember the cry of our Lord on the cross, "My God, why?" So, if the Lord will thus bless us, we will in the sanctuary of our God climb up to that high imminence the psalmist ascended to and we will see as God sees and then will we understand.

God in Suffering

Whatever the providence, however the turn of fortune, God is in it. When you read the Book of Job about all you see is Satan and Satan's oversowing. He covers the horizon from side to side. We see the waste of death, of murder, of blood, of robbery, of violence, affliction, sores, pain, and misery. He seems to color the whole creation. What we sometimes do not remember is that God is there also. There is Someone besides Satan and Satan goes only as far as God permits him. He can do thus, but nothing more. He is allowed so much, but no more. The hound of hell and the dog of damnation can snap and bark, but he has an iron collar around his neck and on that collar is an iron chain and the end of that chain is held by the hand of the omnipotent God. Satan can do just so much and God reins him in. Do not ever forget that the Sovereign of the universe and the Sovereign of history and the Sovereign of national life and the Sovereign of political and state life and the Sovereign of individual life is not damnation and Satan. It is the Lord God almighty. He reigns on His throne, high and lifted up forever. And that chain is in His hand.

Whenever in Scripture the Lord repeats a person's name, be alert. Open your ears. He has something significant to say. "Simon, Simon, Satan has desired to have you that he may thresh you, sift you like wheat poured into a thresher." Simon had once said he loved the Lord with all his heart, and if the whole world were to deny Christ, yet he would not deny Him, so the Lord wanted to talk to him about that. He wanted to let Simon know that he had given Satan permission. He had said yes, but just so far and no further. And when Simon would come back, he would strengthen his brethren. Thus Satan threshed him. Simon Peter swore and denied the Lord. Satan sifted him, threshed him, shook him, but when it was done, there came out of the fire and out of the trial a different Simon Peter. He was a different man.

Peter speaks of this in the fifth chapter of his first epistle: "Humble yourselves therefore under the mighty hand of God, that he may exalt you in due time: casting all your care upon him; for he careth for you." When Satan was done with him, in the permissive will of God, there was a lot of chaff in him that was blown away and a lot of dross in him that was burned out. And the Lord was in it all. So in the life of Job he was sorely tempted but he never failed in his witness to the Lord. Satan has cast him on a dung heap, but he made the dung heap a throne in the presence of the great God. Satan afflicted him with sores and boils, but Job made them signets of honor. They were citations and medals all over him and Job made Satan eat his words. He made Satan confess that he was a liar, and God was in it all. Not only was God in Job's trials, but He also gave Job double of everything he possessed. Satan had a purpose, but he is not the only one who has a purpose. God has a purpose also. And God's purpose was to give Job twice as much as he ever had. Now, to give him twice as many camels and twice as many herds and twice as many fields and twice as many flocks was easy. Some of you have done that yourselves. You have taken what you had and have doubled it. And sometimes you have quadrupled it. It was easy for God to give Job twice as much substance and affluence as he had before. But you see, God does not just think of us in terms of silver or gold or bonds or stocks or lands or herds or flocks or cattle or real estate or things. God purposed to give Job a double of everything he had, including His grace and His love. And to do that, Job had to suffer, for grace and love do not come in any other way than through great trial and great suffering.

Yielded Submission

Job was a man who found greatness in yielded submission, in loss, in pain. He was a man who came to glory under the hand of God. The purpose of the Lord for us is that we might be not only soldiers of the golden fleece, but also soldiers of the iron cross. In the furnace of the fires of the trial of God, the Lord always has a purpose. From that vantage point, looking as God views our sufferings, we see that He is in it, He purposes for us a double portion of His grace and kindness, and He would bring us to glory. Had Job remained a rich man and that is all, would it have been the same? There are thousands of men just like him today. He had thousands of camels. Do they not? Thousands of sheep. Do they not? Thousands of oxen. Do they not? Acres of fields and land. Do they not? Had Job remained just another rich man, you never would have heard of him. Do you not think his friends were also affluent and wealthy? It is customary for friends of like financial situations to gather together. The three men who came to visit Job in his affliction possibly were rich. Did you ever hear of anyone turning to Bildad or Eliphaz or Zophar? James says in our text, "Ye have heard of the patience of Job." I have, so have you. It was the purpose of God to bring Job to glory.

God had a marvelous thought in His mind when He looked at Job and saw how fine he was and how good he was and how responsible he was. So God decided to lift him up, to bless him beyond what Job ever thought possible in just having possessions. God added to Job's possessions a shekinah, a glory, a presence as though it were given from heaven itself. Did you know trial does that and without the trial there is no glory? Abraham is the only man in the Scriptures called "the friend of God" — Abraham. When was Abraham called the friend of God? When the Lord told the old patriarch to take his son to Mt. Moriah, build an altar, bind him, put him on the stone, raise up a knife, plunge it in his heart, and pour out his blood upon the ground. Abraham, not staggering before the promise of God, just trusted against trust, because he was persuaded that God would raise the boy from the dead. He built the altar, bound the lad, lifted up the knife, and in figure received him from the dead. It was the trial that made him great. It is the fury of the furnace that makes the gold pure, and this is God's purpose for us. It is hard for us to say it, but looking at it from God's vantage point, just to be at ease, just to be wealthy, or just to have an abundance of things is, as God says, to be poor. But to be rich toward God, to have experiences of grace, and to trust in God, we need trials and tribulations. What glory God purposes for His people when we endure affliction and trials like the prophets, like the apostles, and like the patriarch — like Job.

God's Revelation to Us

What does God reveal to us when we come into His sanctuary and when we are lifted up and when we see as God sees and we understand as God understands? (1) God is in it all. He has an iron collar and an iron chain on Satan. He can go just so far and not beyond. (2) God purposes for us double everything that we have — double grace, double experience, double love, double everything. (3) God would bring us to glory in our trials. He would refine and purify us. (4) God would through us, as through Job, make us a blessing to others. The Lord put a thorn in Job's neck, He tore up his house of ease, and He pushed him out and over the cliff, just as an eagle does. But over that vast cliff, the blue atmosphere that yawns beneath, the bird learns to fly. God does that for us. He makes us mature and grown up, and we come to the consummation of that *telos*, that end that God has for us in order that we may be a blessing and an encouragement to others.

John Bunyan was an outstanding preacher, a magnificent preacher. But that was all. And people loved to hear him preach. Then God took him and put him in Bedford Prison for twelve years, and out of that Bedford jail was born a glorious book, *Pilgrim's Progress*. It was born in the tears of incarceration. The apostle Paul spent most of his ministry in prison, but out of the imprisonment came the letters that form most of our New Testament. The Lord allowed Jesus to be nailed to the cross, and in suffering and agony there to die, but out of death came life and out of suffering came salvation and out of His burial in the tomb came our promise of a better resurrection.

This is the purpose of God. What befalls you is not unknown to Him. And the sufferings that you experience are not strange in His eyes. He is just bringing you to glory. Blessed are they who endure, who keep their faith, who look up in prayer, who glorify God in suffering or in tears. Blessed are they who look up in faith, who trust Him through it all.

CHAPTER 14

PRAISE AND PROSPERITY
(James 5:11)

As we continue our study of the Epistle of James, we notice how pragmatically he writes. He is where the people are, not in some philosophical, theological world. And he writes about things that we know and experience and things that we ought to do in the household of faith. So, in our text verse we read, "Ye have heard of the patience of Job, and have seen the end of the Lord; that the Lord is very pitiful, and of tender mercy." And what drew my attention to the verse was the word translated as "end." "You have seen the *end* of the Lord." The word is *telos*. Everywhere else in the Bible you will find the word translated "perfect" — *teleios*. And the idea of perfection in the Word is not our concept of sinlessness, without spot or blemish. To us, perfect always means that, but that is not the meaning here. The word *telos, teleios,* means the consummation of a purpose for which a thing was made. It is to arrive. For example, a man is a *telos* or a *teleios* of a boy. The purpose of God for the boy is that he grow to become a man. If he does not, he has not achieved the purpose of God. That is the meaning of the word here.

An Illustration From Job

I was drawn to the text when it spoke about Job and what God did in the consummation of his life. So I turn over to Job 42 and I read what God did for Him. "So the Lord blessed the latter end of Job more than his beginning: for he had fourteen thousand sheep, and six thousand camels, and one thousand yoke of oxen and a thousand she asses. He had also seven sons and three daughters." Is it not remarkable what God did as He brought Job to the consummation of his life? So I look at Job to see what kind of a man he was, and what it was that brought this marvelous blessing and prosperity to his life. In Job 42 the old patriarch cries, "I have heard of thee by the hearing of the ear: but now mine eye seeth thee. Wherefore I abhor myself, and repent in dust and ashes." After that the Lord spoke to Job's comforters and said to them, "My wrath is kindled against thee . . . for ye have not spoken of me the thing that is right and my servant Job hath. Therefore take unto you now seven bullocks and seven rams, and go to my servant Job, and offer up for yourselves a burnt offering; and my servant Job shall pray for you." The Lord turned the captivity of Job when he prayed for his friends, and the Lord gave Job twice as much as he had before. "So the LORD blessed the latter end of Job more than his beginning: for he had fourteen thousand sheep and six thousand camels and one thousand yoke of oxen, and a thousand she asses. He had also seven sons and three daughters." What do you think about that?

This is the life of a man who steadfastly adored and served the Lord. When he was bereft of everything he possessed, he said, "The LORD gave, and the LORD hath taken away; blessed be the name of the LORD." When Satan afflicted him with boils from the top of his head to the bottom of his feet, he said, "Though he slay me, yet will I trust in him." Then, having been brought through those days of terrible disaster and catastrophic loss, and having seen the blessings of God on his life, he said, "I abhor myself, and repent in dust and ashes." God was pleased with the spirit of praise and adoration of Job. God accepted him, was delighted with him, and He gave him twice as much as he had before. That is the thought of our chapter — "Praise and Prosperity." It speaks of our adoration of God, our thanksgiving and gratitude to Him and His infinite blessings to us.

AN ILLUSTRATION FROM THE LEVITICAL LAW

Did you notice in reading about this *teleios* of Job, that it spoke of these offerings — seven bullocks and seven rams offered up to God? Let us take a look at the Levitical law and at the sacrifices the people brought before the Lord. In the Book of Leviticus we read of five offerings. Looking at those five offerings, we notice that two of them were mandatory. It was necessary that the worshiper bring those offerings in worship. One was the sin offering and the other like it, the trespass offering. The sin offering because of sins against God, and the trespass offering because of sins against other people and against holy things. Both of them were similar. They were sin offerings. No man can come before God without the shedding of blood, for without the shedding of blood there is no remission of sins. And in the Old Testament, by type, they sacrificed an innocent animal, poured out its blood, and in the blood sacrifice came before the Lord. Today we come before God in the blood of the cross, pleading the propitiation, the atonement, the pouring out of the crimson of our Lord's life on the cross. No man shall ever stand in the presence of God in his sin. He must find atonement, and atonement means the shedding of blood.

The other three offerings were called sweet savor offerings. What do we mean by a sweet savor offering? It was an offering where the smoke of the offering ascended heavenward, and if the fragrance of it delighted God it was called a sweet savor offering. Now, those offerings — burnt, peace, and meal — were called sweet savor offerings because they were not commanded. The individual came before God and brought his offerings to the Lord because he loved Him, and it was a way of praising God and giving thanks to Him.

Now I am going to change the wording of one of these offerings so you can see it more perfectly. What the Bible calls a peace offering we would call today a praise offering, a thanksgiving offering. Practically all of the offerings of the tabernacle and of the temple were peace offerings. They were thanksgiving offerings. Few of them were burnt offerings. Offerings were presented out of gratitude and the overflowing praise and thanksgiving of the heart. The offerer would gather his family together, and whatever friends he would invite, and the offering was sacrificed before God and was shared as a communal meal. It was a thanksgiving dinner, a thanksgiving sacrifice. It was brought to the house of the Lord, the ministers shared it, and God looked upon it and called it a fragrant offering, a sweet savor offering.

The Life of Praise

There is something marvelous about this. There was a presupposition on the part of God that the life of His people would be a life of praise, and of gladness and thanksgiving, that the overflowing gratitude of their hearts and the love of their deepest souls for God would find expression in these offerings of praise and gratitude. You will find that overflowing spirit reflected in the life of the people. For example, look at Psalm 96. "O sing unto the Lord a new song: sing unto the Lord, all the earth. Sing unto the Lord, bless his name; shew forth His salvation from day to day. Declare his glory among the heathen, his wonders among all the people. . . . Give unto the Lord the glory due unto his name: bring an offering and come into his courts. . . . Let the heavens rejoice, and let the earth be glad; let the sea roar, and the fulness thereof. . . . Before the Lord: for he cometh to judge the earth." That is the spirit of overflowing praise on the part of the people. Praise His name. Give glory due the Lord. Bring an offering and come into His courts. Let us also observe Psalm 150. "Praise ye the Lord. Praise God in his sanctuary: praise him in the firmament of his power. Praise him for his mighty acts: praise him according to his excellent greatness. Praise him with the sound of the trumpet: praise him with the psaltery and harp. Praise him with the timbrel and dance: praise him with stringed instruments and organs. Praise him upon the loud cymbals: praise him upon the high sounding cymbals. Let every thing that hath breath praise the Lord. Praise ye the Lord."

What does it mean to praise Him with the timbrel and dance? When a man is so full of praise and gratitude to God he cannot contain himself, and he stands up before the Lord and walks before Him with words of praise, with shouts of gladness and glory, that is what the psalmist means. In 2 Samuel 6, the story is told of David bringing the ark into Jerusalem and how, when the ark was brought into Jerusalem, David sang before God with all his might. It was a hallelujah occasion. It was a great hour. We are not moved like that much any more, but when I grew up as a boy I used to see people moved like that. And in the beginning of my ministry, I used to see people like that. I was invited as a young man to hold a revival meeting in a church. That morning two young men were saved. And when time came for the pastor to introduce them to the church, a young woman stood up and asked the pastor if she could say something. She was the teacher, I found out, of a Bible class in the church. She came forward and put one of her hands on the head of one of those boys and said that on that day she praised God for one of her boys. Then she took her other hand and put it on the head of the other lad and told how God was better to her than her prayer. That day God had given her both of her boys. And then from one side to the other of that beautiful church she shouted and clapped her hands and praised God. You never felt such a thing. The vast throng that jammed the church that morning was bowed as one in tears of gratitude and thanksgiving.

That is what Psalm 150 refers to. How wonderful it is! How marvelous it is to feel it. The glory of it. You become so full of the praise and gratitude of God that you have to shout it. That is the presupposition of that offering of sweet savor, that out of the gratitude of the hearts of the people there would be a voluntary offering — not one that commanded, but something that came out of the fullness of their hearts.

Praise and Gratitude in Giving

How do you give in gratitude? Do you give to someone because you must or because you want to? Do you give because there is a need only? This is good but would it not be better to give to someone when there is no need or give them something they do not need? A man may give his wife a new iron because her old one broke and she needs a new one. But think how much better and sweeter to give to his wife a pretty new dress. The gift should be given out of gratitude and thanksgiving. God calls that a sweet savor offering. It has a fragrance that pleases God.

There are some things that are commanded us of God in the Bible. One is that a man owes a tithe to the Lord. From the days of the patriarchs like Abraham and Jacob through all of the Levitical legislation, the tithe was holy to the Lord. And this applies to this present day as we read in Hebrews 7. I owe a tithe to God. That belongs to Him. And when a man does the commandment of God, He says He willl bless him for it. Malachi tells us that if I give my tithe to the Lord He "will open the windows (plural) of heaven, and pour you out a blessing" I cannot contain. I owe my tithe to God and when I give it God will bless me. What of the offering of necessity? God will bless it. What of the offering of commandment? God will bless it. But oh, the richness and the glory of coming before God with a sweet savor offering. "This I give, Lord, out of the fullness of my heart." This is of praise and gratitude. God says it is fragrant and beautiful in His sight.

CHAPTER 15

DIVINE HEALING
(James 5:13-16)

I would like to discuss with you the concept of "divine healing." James writes of this in 5:13-16: "Is any among you afflicted? let him pray. Is any merry? let him sing psalms. Is any sick among you? let him call for the elders of the church; and let them pray over him, anointing him with oil in the name of the Lord: And the prayer of faith shall save the sick, and the Lord shall raise him up; and if he have committed sins, they shall be forgiven him. Confess your faults one to another, and pray one for another, that ye may be healed." Let us take a look at the passage for a moment. "Is any sick among you? let him call for the elders of the church." We would use the word "pastors" of the church. Three words refer to the office of a pastor. One of the words is translated as "elder," referring to the honor of the office. Another means "bishop," which refers to the assignment, the responsibility of the office. And the third one means "shepherd," which refers to his pastoral care of the congregation. But all three words are used interchangeably of the same office. They refer to the same man, whether he is called an elder, a bishop or a pastor, or a shepherd — it is all the same man in the New Testament. So if one is sick, let him call for the "pastors" of the church and let them pray over him, "anointing him with oil in the name of the Lord: and the prayer of faith shall save the sick."

PRAYER AND HEALING

James says the prayer *shall* heal him and the Lord *shall* raise him up and if he has committed sins they *shall* be forgiven him. James is saying that if the illness is caused by his own wrongdoing or if it is not

Divine Healing

caused by his own wrongdoing, either way, his sins shall be forgiven him. In the praying and anointing the man is not only healed in his physical frame, but he also is healed in his heart and soul. He is forgiven.

What does this praying and this anointing with oil refer to? I suppose that if you had a dozen commentaries at your disposal, you might come up with a dozen different interpretations. For example, Ellicott's Commentary, one of the finest, says that this anointing with oil is just symbolic. It has no medicinal efficacy at all. If you read the American Commentary on the New Testament, which is a Baptist commentary published by the Judson Press in Philadelphia, you read that this anointing with oil is medicinal. It is medicine to help the man get well. Now, one of the great commentaries of all time is called the *Expositor's Bible,* and on one page of the *Expositor's Bible* it says one thing and on the other page it says something diametrically opposite. I mention this to show you the differences of interpretation regarding this verse. Well, we are going to look at it just as the Bible presents it to us. Divine healing — the minister praying and anointing with oil.

Psychology and Healing

One thing that is certain is the psychological implication. It is good to do something to help people believe they can be well. In the story of our Lord when He healed the blind man He made a clay of spittle and anointed the eyes of the man and he was healed. On another occasion He touched the ears of a deaf man and he could hear. It helped the man's faith to have some token of its healing. Did you know that there are healing properties in saliva? Have you ever wondered how the inside of your mouth heals when it is wet all the time? God put a healing property in the saliva and it will heal. You sometimes see this illustrated when a dog licks his sores. So, for Christ to use a means like saliva helps man's faith that he will be well.

Oil and Wine and Healing

We also see that oil and sometimes wine were used in healing and medicinal purposes. In Isaiah 1:6 Isaiah speaks of the wounds of the people that have not been healed with oil, with ointment. And in the beautiful story of the good Samaritan, the man who fell among the thieves and was left wounded and for dead, the kind Samaritan picked him up and poured into his wounds oil and wine. Medicinally, he ministered to the man who was so grievously hurt. In classical literature, Deo Cassius and Strabo describe the army of Gallius as being afflicted with a malady and they ministered to the soldiers with a mixture of oil and wine, externally and internally. Josephus, in describing the death of Herod the Great, said the physicians bathed his body in oil.

MEANS AND HEALING

However that worked, there are two things in our text that are very plain. (1) The prayer of faith will heal the sick and the Lord will raise him up. (2) There are means that are used in that healing. What of this healing of our bodies? One day I was walking down one of the corridors in Baylor Hospital and a man stopped me and asked me a question that I have been asked many times. Because of a serious illness in his family, he asked me if I believed in divine healing. I asked him if there was any other kind. Does anyone heal but God? The doctor can prescribe and the surgeon can cut and the physician can sew up the wound, but it is God who heals. The pharmacist cannot heal, the physician cannot heal, the surgeon cannot heal. Only God can heal. And the surgeon, the doctor, and the pharmacist are as helpless before God as you and I are. They have to depend upon God, whether they admit it or not. The physician may be an infidel or an atheist, but he has to depend upon God for healing. There is no other kind of healing but divine healing. It comes from the gracious hands of the Lord.

Someone may ask, Do we have a right to look to God for healing and to expect it from His bountiful hands? The answer to that is an affirmative yes. By the Holy Scriptures, we have a right to ask God for healing. In Exodus 15 the Lord says to His people, "My name is, I am the LORD that healeth thee." That is one of God's names. Look at Matthew 8: "When the even was come, they brought unto him many that were possessed with devils: and he cast out the spirits with his word, and healed all that were sick: that it might be fulfilled which was spoken by Esaias the prophet, saying, Himself took our infirmities, and bare our sicknesses," quoting Isaiah 53:4.

A part of the atonement of Christ is for the healing of our bodies. His atonement was not only for the forgiveness of our sins, but also for the healing of our bodies. In Romans 8:11 Paul writes, "But if the

Divine Healing

Spirit of him that raised up Jesus from the dead dwell in you, he that raised up Christ from the dead shall also quicken your mortal bodies by his Spirit that dwelleth in you." The text does not say your dead bodies. It says your mortal bodies. That is, your bodies that are liable to pain and suffering and illness. The spirit of Christ that dwells in you heals you, quickens you, brings you to strength and to health.

Now we find in the Word of God instance after instance of God's divine graciousness in healing His people. Abraham prayed for Abimelech and God healed him. Moses prayed for his sister, Miriam, who was stricken with leprosy, and God healed her. Hezekiah prayed before the Lord and God heard his prayer and healed him. And in the New Testament, in the life of Christ and the apostles, we see this illustrated often. There were those who were healed by the gracious hand of our Lord and by the gifts of the Spirit in the apostles. So by the Word of the Lord, I have a right, a privilege to go before God and to ask for healing.

Also, does God use means in healing? Are there instruments, are there medicines? Are there procedures, are there ways that God uses to heal us? Yes. For example, one of the noblest stories in the Bible concerns good King Hezekiah. The Lord sent him word and told him to set his house in order, for he was going to die. And King Hezekiah turned his face to the wall, prayed and wept, and Isaiah was sent to Hezekiah with the word that the Lord had heard his prayers and seen his tears, and He would add fifteen years to his life. That is a beautiful story of God's healing. Isaiah 38:21 has a little addendum to the story. "For Isaiah had said, Let them take a lump of figs, and lay it for a plaster upon the boil, and he shall recover." There were means that were used in the healing of Hezekiah.

Now look at Mark 6:12,13: "And [the disciples] went out, and preached that men should repent. And they cast out many devils, and anointed with oil many that were sick and healed them." The oil was medicinal and the apostles not only went out and preached, but they also healed, using means for the healing.

Let me give you another illustration. In Paul's first letter to his young son in the ministry, Timothy, he writes to the fact that Timothy was weak and sickly. Paul says, "Drink no longer water, but use a little wine for thy stomach's sake and thine often infirmities." Alcohol is so vital to the pharmacist, that medicine would almost be impossible without it. It is one of the finest solutions in which the medicinal efficacies can be dissolved. And that is what Paul writes to his young son in the ministry. Why did Paul not just pray for him that he would get well? Because God has given means to be used to get well. "Use a little wine for thy stomach's sake." Apparently Timothy was a teetotaler and would not touch alcohol. So I learn from the Word of the Lord that when I am sick, I am not only to pray, but I also am to use means that I might be healed.

In Acts 28, when Paul is shipwrecked upon Melita, the beloved physician Luke is with him. Now look at the story. "And it came to pass, that the father of Publius (Publius was the governor of the island) lay sick of a fever and of a bloody flux: to whom Paul entered in, and prayed, and laid his hands on him, and healed him. So when this was done, others also, which had diseases in the island, came, and were healed: Who also honoured us." Paul, the apostle who prayed, and Luke, the beloved physician who practiced medicine, they honored "with many honours; and when we departed, they laded us with such things as were necessary" for their continuing journey. Read that verse over again. Paul laid his hands on a man and healed him. Others who had diseases came also and they were *therapeuo* — the practice of medicine was carried out on them. Is there anything wrong with that? No. Does that please God? Was the Lord honored in that? Yes. Paul prayed and laid his hands upon them and Luke, the "beloved physician," practiced medicine on them. Do I think that is right? When I read in the Word of God that in the sickness of the people Paul prayed and Luke the beloved physician practiced medicine, I see it in conformity with the whole will and purpose of God. If one is sick, let us pray. There is divine healing in prayer. People are sick in their hearts and in their souls as much as they are in their physical frames. Let us ask God for His healing and then let us use all of the means that we can, for they also are of God. Where did penicillin come from? God made it. It was from the beginning. It is just now we have discovered it. Where do all of these herbs and chemicals come from? They come from the creative hand of God. And for us to have a minister pray for us, and to have friends and neighbors and family pray for us, and for us to have the hospital and the pharmacist and the physician and the surgeon to help us, this is in keeping with the Word of the Lord.

God and Healing

Does God always heal? No. God has healed, God does heal, God can heal, God will heal, but God does not always heal. God told Moses he could not enter the Promised Land. He would die in the land of Moab. Moses pleaded with the Lord and so insistent was his intercession that God told Moses to speak no more to Him of the matter. He would die in the land of Moab. He could not enter in. God does not always heal or add to our days. There comes a time when the sentence of death that is passed upon all mankind passes also upon us in the will of the Lord. Paul came before the Lord with a thorn in his flesh and asked God to remove it and God said no. "My grace is sufficient for thee," and Paul, being a great Christian, said, "Most gladly therefore will I rather glory in my infirmities . . . for when I am weak, then am I strong." It is in my weakness that God perfects His strength. Not always does God heal.

"Divine Healers"

One of the strangest things that I hear constantly comes from divine healers who make money off the illnesses of the people. You put a $100 bill in the collection plate or in an envelope and they will pray and you will get well. That goes on day and night. And they do that on the assumption that they have the gifts of healing. They say the apostles had that. Listen. The only thing the apostles had was the gift and the power of the Spirit to confirm the Word and that was all. They did not have the power to heal indiscriminately. No. Paul writes to Timothy in his last letter saying, "Trophimus have I left at Miletum sick." Why did Paul not heal him? Because he did not have the power to heal him. Why did Paul not heal Epaphroditus who came to see him from Philippi? Because he did not have the power to heal him. The sign, the miracle, was an affirmation of the truth of the word that was preached. But no apostle had the power to heal indiscriminately. "Trophimus have I left at Miletum sick." It may be God's will that I not be well.

Our Attitudes Toward Sickness and Healing

Now let us look at another thought regarding illness. What is to be the attitude of a child of God toward illness? We must accept the fact that illness, disease, germs, bacteria — these things that hurt us and cause us to be sick — they are here, along with the accidents that we fall into. And death is here and we cannot deny it. One of the strangest, to me, of all of the denominations is the one that denies the reality of hurt and injury and disease and illness. They say it is just in the mind — there is no such thing as hurt or illness or disease. And at the same time they are saying it, they may have mouths full of crockery and eyes covered with heavy lenses. But there is just no such thing as disease — it is just in the mind. I once was a pastor of a church in a town where there was a university. The mother of one of the professors in the university was a devout Baptist and belonged to our congregation. She was a big, heavy woman and one day she stumbled and fell down the steps into the basement. She was bruised from head to foot. The daughter ran down and helped her mother up and told her she was not hurt. "You're not hurt. That's just in your mind." No doctor was called, no pharmacist was contacted for medication. I went out to see that mother. She was lying in her bed in pain and was black and blue all over. She was hurt and hurting. But not to her daughter. It was all in her mother's mind.

There are times when I am sick — that is just a fact. And the best thing for me to do is to recognize it. So what do I do with my illnesses and with my hurts? Having recognized them, I talk to God and take it to Him. My suffering may be my own fault. I may eat the wrong things and get sick. I may have the wrong diet and get sick. I may not observe the laws of health and get sick. So I should search for the reason why I am ill.

Also, suffering can be a chastening from the Lord. In Hebrews 13 we are told that whom the Lord loves He chastens. And if we are not chastened, we are not children of God. It could be due to something we have done that is not right. Illness can be an affliction and a judgment from God. A rampaging illness that is scourging America today, and especially our teenagers, is due to the promiscuity, the immorality of our young people. The doctors do not know what to do in many places because it is becoming epidemic. There are illnesses that are due to our sins and are judgments from almighty God.

Again, it may be that we are afflicted that we might manifest the glory of the Lord. The disciples passed by and saw a man blind from birth. And they asked the Lord who sinned, the man or his parents that he should be born blind. The Lord said the man was born blind

Divine Healing

not because of his sin or the sin of his parents, but that the glory of God might be made manifest in him. There are illnesses that are sent upon us that we might demonstrate to the world the glory, the manifested presence of almighty God. Job had that experience. His "friends" tried to convince him that he was a great sufferer because he was a great sinner. Not so. God told the three friends that they did not speak right concerning Him. They were to go to Job and ask Job to pray for them, lest they die. There are some things that God sends upon us that we are to bear for the glory of the Lord.

My predecessor at the First Baptist Church of Dallas was Dr. George Truett. For a full year before he died, Dr. Truett suffered agonizingly. He was allergic to all pain-killing drugs. Any narcotic would make him deathly sick — nauseated. So he suffered excruciating pain for a full year. Many who loved him would ask me again and again why it was that Dr. Truett, the great man of God and the incomparable preacher of the Word, had to suffer so much for a full year. But Dr. Truett had a secret. His faith in the Lord and in the goodness of God was gigantic and he repeated so many times that which he preached so often, "Not my will, but thine be done." In that faith and in that yielded submissiveness, the great pastor died. That is what it is to be a Christian. Anyone can sing songs and be happy when all is well. But what happens when the dark day comes, when the valley stretches endlessly ahead, when illness racks, and the bed is itself an affliction? That is when we glorify God, singing songs in the night, trusting in the goodness of the Lord. We take it to God in prayer, and ask the pastor and people who believe in the Lord to pray. We use every means God has given us — the doctor, the pharmacist, the hospital — then having prayed, having done all that we know how to do, yielded, submissive, we leave the final verdict in God's hands. If it is God's will that we live, may we praise the Lord in the gift of days. If it is God's will that our lives be closed like a book and the last chapter be written, then may we have the faith to believe that God will heal us over there. This is what it is to be a Christian.

CHAPTER 16

EFFECTUAL PRAYING
(James 5:13-18)

Have you ever heard of "effectual praying"? The effectual, fervent prayer of a righteous man? Look at James 5:13,14. "Is any among you afflicted? let him pray. Is any merry? let him sing psalms. Is any sick among you? let him call for the elders of the church; and let them pray over him, anointing him with oil in the name of the Lord." These verses speak of prayer and means. All of the pharmaceutical gifts that heal us, God gave to us. We are to pray and to use means. "And the prayer of faith shall save the sick, and the Lord shall raise him up; and if he have committed sins, they shall be forgiven him. Confess your faults one to another, and pray one for another, that ye may be healed." And now for the theme of this chapter: "The effectual fervent prayer of a righteous man availeth much."

Prayer and Means

Elijah was a man subject to like passions as we are. He prayed earnestly that it might not rain and it did not rain on the earth for three and one-half years. He prayed again and the heavens gave rain and the earth brought forth her fruit. It is only an atheist who does not pray, and at times even he will be forced to his knees to call upon the name of God. But all of God's people should find prayer as natural in their lives as it is to breathe or to eat or to drink or to lie down and sleep. The man who belongs to God will pray, especially when he comes to crisis in his life. Recently one of the beloved members of my church came to see me and told me she faced a severe operation. She wondered if I would pray with her. This is the natural reaction of a child of God — to pray.

Effectual Praying

God made it that way when He put the world together and put us together in it. It was a part of the program of the Lord that we ask, that we talk to God, that we bare our souls open and naked before Him. He does what He does in the universe without any intercession, without any appeal on our part. I guess God could have put us together in a home where we would never talk to each other, but it would be a strange thing since God has made us to talk to each other. It is the same thing about God and His creation. God made it where we would talk to each other. In fact, I think if a man preached on Genesis and said that God created man and his wife for fellowship with the Lord, someone whom God could talk to and Someone to whom they could talk I think he would have good exegesis of the matter. I do not think mountains and oceans and stars and seas and continents particularly thrill God, but I think talking to Him does and loving Him does and praying to Him does.

The Bible has a beautiful imagery of how God looks upon our praying. It is the imagery of a sweet savor, a fragrance that mounts upward to God. You find this all through the Bible. Had you entered the holy place, the sanctuary of the Lord in the tabernacle or the temple, on the left side you would have found the seven-branch golden candlestick. On the right side you would have found the golden table of shewbread, but in the center you would have found the altar of prayer. It was situated just before the veil, and when the priest went in he went in with incense and burned it on that golden altar. And while the people prayed outside in the courtyard, the fragrance of the incense mounted upward to God. All of this is a picture, an image of how God looks upon our praying.

In the fifth chapter of the Book of Revelation we see the dramatic presentation of the Lamb of God, the lion of the tribe of Judah, prevailing to take the book of redemption out of the hand of him who sat upon the throne and to open the seals thereof and to look upon the pages. When He, the Lord Christ, had taken the book, the four cherubim and the four and twenty elders fell down before the Lamb, every one of them having harps and golden vials full of odors, fragrances, which were the prayers of the saints. Now turn to Revelation 8. "And another angel came and stood at the altar, having a golden censer; and there was given unto him much incense, that he should offer it with the prayers of all saints upon the golden altar which was before the throne. And the smoke of the incense, which came with the prayers of the saints, ascended up before God out of the angel's hand." The imagery is all through the Holy Scriptures. Our praying is like fragrance that comes up to the Lord and the sweet savor of it delights God in heaven.

There is an old Talmudic legend about Sandalfond, the angel of prayer. And the story of his assignment has been written in verse.

> Standing erect at the outermost gates
> Of the city celestial he waits
> With his feet on the ladder of light.
> Listening breathless to the sounds that ascend from below.
>
> From the spirits on earth that adore,
> From the souls that entreat and implore
> In the fervor and passion of prayer.
> From the hearts that are broken with losses
> And weary with dragging their crosses
> Too heavy for mortals to bear.
>
> And he gathers the prayers as he stands
> And they change to flowers in his hands.
> Into garlands of purple and red.
> And beneath the great arch of the portal,
> Through the streets of the City Immortal
> Is wafted the fragrance they shed.

Is that not a beautiful sentiment? So biblical. Our prayers ascend up to heaven and as the angel presents them before God they are turned into fragrances like beautiful flowers. And there they come up before God in beautiful, precious intercession.

Earnest Prayer

Now the illustration that the pastor uses is a tremendous one. "The effectual fervent prayer of a righteous man availeth much." Let us look at Elijah again. He prayed earnestly that it might not rain, and it did not rain for three and one-half years. Then he prayed again, no less earnestly, and the heaven gave her rain and the earth brought forth her fruit. He was certainly a man of passions. This mountain of a man with a whirlwind of heaven in his heart was volitive, he was eruptive. In a passion of anger he stood before Ahab and Jezebel. In a passion of contempt and scorn he ridiculed the false prophets of Baal and Baal himself. In a passion and fury he destroyed the places and the high scenes of idolatry in Israel. In a passion of intercession and prayer he asked God for rain upon the thirsting earth. In a passion of ecstasy he ran before the chariot of Ahab from Carmel to Jezreel, a distance of thirty miles. And in a like passion of despondency and melancholia he ran from Jezebel, and sat in grief and despair under a juniper tree. He was certainly a man of passions. But he was at the same time a mysterious man. He would suddenly appear before Ahab and just as suddenly go away. He would suddenly appear before Obadiah and just as suddenly be gone. He would suddenly appear before Ahaziah and his companies of fifty and then just as quickly disappear. He suddenly appeared before Elisha, then before his very eyes was carried away into glory. How does the Old Testament end? "Behold, I will send you Elijah the prophet, before the coming of the great and dreadful day of the LORD."

When I turn the page, having seen how the Old Testament closes with Elijah, I see that Matthew also speaks of him. And John the Baptist, going in the power and spirit of Elijah, announces the coming of the kingdom. In Matthew 17, when the Lord is speaking to His disciples concerning His coming, the disciples reply, "Master, it is our understanding that Elijah shall precede the coming of the Messiah." And He answered them, "Elijah truly must come and restore all things, but I say unto you that Elijah has already come and they did not know him. They did with him what they wanted and cut off his head. Then the disciples understood that He spake to them of John the Baptist."

This man Elijah closed the Old Testament, opened the New Testament, and some believe that when the Lord Jesus comes again He will be preceded by the return of the prophet Elijah. What a mountain of a man. Great, solitary, stalwart, standing for God in a day and an age of absolute apostasy, like America is in today. The time was corrupt and evil and becoming more so with the passing of every hour. And alone he gave himself as a champion for God for revival, for turning the people back to the Lord God.

BOLDNESS IN PRAYER

I cannot help but pause here to remark on the fearlessness of God's saints. When a man is full of the Holy Ghost he is bold and fearless before anyone, upon any occasion in the earth. I read for example as I prepared this chapter about Francis of Assisi and how in 1219 he journeyed with a few of his disciples to Egypt to present the cause of Christ, to preach the gospel to the Islamic world. He stood before Kameel, the sultan of Egypt, to present the claims of Christ. The bold fearlessness of the man, and his deep Christian humility made a profound impression upon the sultan. One day Francis was appealing to the sultan. As he spoke, a decree came from the priest of Mohammed and was addressed to the sultan. It said, "Sire, you are learned in the law and you are sworn to uphold it by the hand of Mohammed, the prophet of God. And we are asking you, therefore, to take off the heads of these men." When the request was made, Francis of Assisi replied, "Sire, I have tried to get your priests to talk to me and they will not do it. Maybe they will act for you." He went on and said, "Cause a great fire to be built. Heat the furnace seven times hotter than usual, and I and my disciples will enter the fire. Cause the priests of Islam also to enter the fire, and we shall see whose faith is true and whose God answers prayer." By the time Francis had finished his address and had presented his challenge, the priests of Islam, horrified at the thought, silently slunk away. And Francis was left standing by himself with his little handful of Christian followers. The sultan looked around, and seeing all of the Islamic devotees gone said, "It must be that my priests worship with words and not by faith." That is the stuff God's saints are made of. We may not have many such today, but they have been innumerable in days past and Elijah was one of them. Fearless and bold, he prayed that God would withhold rain from the earth. Why that? Because the people needed to come back to the God upon whom their lives and living depended.

Persistent Prayer

We too must remember that it is God who gives us breath. It is God who gives us length of days. It is God who sends the rain. It is God who makes the germinating seed to sprout and gives us fruit and fertility and increase and abundance. Our lives are dependent upon God, and in order to show that dependence, Elijah prayed that the Lord would withhold rain from the earth, and God listened to a man pray. The earth turned to iron and the heavens turned to brass. The cold stars looked down from the sky and there was no dew. The watercourses were dried up and there was no vegetation. The earth,

Effectual Praying

burned and dry, cracked into great fissures. Even the brook Cherith, where Elijah was fed by the ravens, dried up, and the whole earth cried and moaned in its grief, and the people suffered in their poverty and famine and death. After three and one-half years Elijah, the man of God, knelt once again before the Lord and prayed, and this time he asked the Lord to open the windows of heaven and send showers and rain from His gracious hands. He prayed six times and there was no answer. And when he prayed the seventh time his servant came back from looking out over the great sea from the top of Mt. Carmel and brought the announcement that he saw over the sea a cloud the size of a man's hand. When God helps He helps mightily. When God sends an advance guard, the great battalions are following, and Elijah stood up and told Ahab to get going because there would be an abundance of rain. God answered a man's prayer and brought refreshing rain upon the thirsting earth.

Pray Always

But you say that's no illustration for you. How could you ever mount up in fearless faith like Elijah? To compare you with Elijah is no illustration at all. And to talk to you about prayer as we speak here concerning Elijah means nothing to you. You are not in the same world. How could that be an encouragement to you? Well, James was the pastor of the church and he lived among his people and he knew them well. He knew they might say something like this, so that is the reason he wrote as he did: He says Elijah was a man subject to like passions as we are. He had feelings such as we have, sometimes exulted, sometimes cast down. The word *homoiopathais*, "of like nature," is used in the fourteenth chapter of the Book of Acts. Paul and Barnabas had healed the lame man at Lystra, and the people came out to offer sacrifices, saying that the gods had come down to earth in the likeness of men; and when Paul saw it, he rent his garments, telling them they were only *homoiopathais*. They were men of like living, like failing, like passions as the rest. That is what James says here about the prophet. He was a man like us. He prayed in the hour of need. In the poor home of Zarephath when the widow's son died, Elijah prayed, and God heard his prayer and restored the son to the arms of his mother. He was a man just as we are, but he prayed.

Prayer and Righteousness

Now there were two ways that he prayed and both of those ways are ours for the having. Look to the text. "The effectual, fervent prayer of a righteous man availeth much." First notice the phrase "a righteous man." God has deference to a righteous man. A righteous man cannot talk to God and God not hear him and heed him. God listens. When Abraham stood before the Lord and He told Abraham He was going to destroy the cities of the plain, Abraham asked God to spare the city if there were fifty righteous people in it. The Lord said He would. Then Abraham went down, forty, thirty, twenty, ten. And the reason Abraham stopped at ten is because he took it for granted that Lot, his family, and the friends he would have won to the Lord in that length of time would have spared the city. But there were not even ten. Had there been ten, Sodom and Gomorrah would not have been destroyed. God listens to a righteous man. And when a man who is righteous before God, who comes in the blood of Christ and in the forgiveness of sin, stands before God and pleads his cause, God listens to him. The Book says so.

Fervent Prayer

Also notice that the prayer is to be "fervent." The two Greek words used are *polu* and *isquai* and mean "much strong." The "much strong" prayer of a righteous man is *energao* "energy." Thus, prayer from a righteous man offered to God earnestly, fervently, has energy in it. God did it that way. A tiny, invisible atom has more energy in it than anything else in this earth. Who put it there? God did. And God put energy in prayer. If you want power in the church, pray. If you want power in the pulpit, pray. If you want power in the nation, pray. If you want power in the work, pray. There's *energao* in it. Just as God has done with the atom — there's more power in it than anything we can do. We can work and work but it's not half as effective as to pray and pray. We go farthest when we go on our knees.

Chapter 17

THE WINNER OF SOULS
(James 5:19, 20)

We have come to the last two verses of the Epistle of James where the discussion centers on the winning of souls. "Brethren, if any of you do err from the truth, and one convert him; let him know, that he which converteth the sinner from the error of his way shall save a soul from death, and shall hide a multitude of sins." Is that not a strong and poignant way to place the truth of God? The winner of souls saves a person from death and hides a multitude of sins. Now we know from the Scriptures that only God can save. He alone can raise us from the dead; He alone can forgive our sins; He alone can write our names in the Lamb's Book of Life. It is God who regenerates the soul — salvation belongs to the Lord. But at the same time, the Scriptures avow that we also do it. In God's hands we are the instruments of God's salvation.

Our Part in Man's Salvation

For an example let us look at Paul as he writes to his young son in the ministry, Timothy, who is now pastor of the church at Ephesus. He tells him to take heed, to himself and to doctrine. "Continue in them: for in doing this thou shalt both save thyself, and them that hear thee." Timothy, if you will be true to the faith and preach the doctrine, the teaching of the Lord, you will save yourself. But what is more, you will save those who hear you. What a glorious encouragement to a pastor and a preacher. If a man will be faithful to the faith, to the doctrine, and preach the Lord, he will save himself and he will save others. That is why it is so unthinkable to me that a minister would stand in the pulpit and preach something else. There are some who preach about economics, about current events, about politics, about all the social issues that frustrate us. You could listen to a commentator on the radio, and he would do the same thing. You could read an editorial, and it would concern itself with the same thing. But the minister is called of God to deliver the Word of the Lord, the Word that can save our souls from death and can forgive our sins and present us some day to God in heaven. Is there a word from the Lord? Is there a doctrine or a teaching from Him? That is the great mandate and assignment of the minister of Christ, for in doing this, the apostle avows, he will both save himself and those who hear him. The man listening is saved, for faith cometh by hearing and hearing by the word of the Lord. So God saves us, but we also do it.

If you know a man who is married to an unsaved woman or a woman married to an unsaved man, tell them not to break up their home. Who knows? The wife could help save her husband, or the husband his wife. The Lord has a part and we have a part. God does it and we do it. It is like a man walking to the edge of a deep abyss, and just as he is about to step over the precipitous cliff, a man seeing him calls to him and saves him from death. In testifying the man says to a friend that the other man saved him from an awful death. Then later at a prayer service in a testimony service the man stands up and he says he was saved from death by the gracious goodness and providence of God. Both of them did it. I remember a young unsaved doctor who joined a clinic in which the elder doctor was a devout Christian. He prayed for the young man and won him to the Lord. In a service at the church the young doctor stood up and in his testimony said, "I was saved by the pastor's sermon on John 6:37 and by the tears of this doctor." God does it, and we do it. "If any one of you err from the truth, and one convert him; let him know, that he which converteth the sinner from the error of his way shall save a soul from death and shall hide a multitude of sins."

The Tragedy of a Lost Soul

We now look at the text a section at a time. First, a reference is made to the greatest tragedy that can overwhelm and overtake a man's life — that his soul die and he be buried beneath a multitude of sins. You see, life in the Bible refers not to existence but to our communion with God. Life in the Bible is our being joined to God.

The Winner of Souls

Death in the Bible is not non-existence, but it refers to our separation from God. Paul mentions in Ephesians 2:1 "you . . . who were dead in trespasses and in sins." He says the man is walking among us, but says he is dead in trespasses and sins. That is, he's away from God. His soul is dead. In 1 Timothy Paul again refers to this. "She that liveth in pleasure is dead while she liveth" (5:6). The woman is a harlot. She is very much alive, but the Book says she is dead. Dead in pleasure, in sin. She is separated from God. The first death in the Bible is the separation between the soul and the body, but the second death is the separation of the soul from God. And that is the greatest tragedy that can happen to a person. Oh, the awesome, sad, and terrible words that are used to describe that estate of a man whose soul is shut out from God. It is a place where the worm does not die and the fire is not quenched. It is called a place where the smoke of their torment ascends forever. It is described as an agony where one cries for a drop of water to cool the tongue tormented in that flame. That is why we sing, "Worthy is the Lamb who was slain, who hath redeemed us," that is, who has bought us, brought us, saved us from so awesome a tragedy. We shall never know the wrath of God. Christ has intervened. We shall never be separated from the Lord. He has joined us to God. Nor shall we ever know the agonies of suffering in the eternal torment and damnation because He has died to save us.

The Joy of Saving a Soul

Therefore, let man know that he who converts the sinner saves that soul and hides a multitude of sins. This is the greatest assignment he could accept. The greatest work one could ever do would be to save a soul from death. If you were on a sinking ship and were able to man the lifeboat, how blessed it would be to save by the lifeboat. If a house were burning down and you dashed through the flames to rescue the perishing, how blessed the act. But it cannot compare to saving a soul from death. In the last century someone asked the famous preacher and scholar, Lyman Beecher, what was the greatest thing that a man could ever do for someone else. Mr. Beecher replied, "To bring another to Jesus. And that is according to the Word of the Lord. In the judgment of God there is nothing so marvelously great as to bring someone to Jesus. The wisest man who ever lived wrote this proverb: "He that winneth souls is wise." If a man is wise in his own conceit, he is contemptible. If he is wise in the wisdom of the world he is acceptable. But if a man is wise in the judgment of God, he is of all people blessed. Did not Daniel write it like that? "And they that be wise shall shine as the brightness of the firmament, and they that turn many to righteousness as the stars for ever and ever" (Dan. 12:3). We see this example in Christ and the apostles. The greatest thing they ever did was to bring souls to our Lord. John the Baptist pointed out the Savior by saying, "Behold the Lamb of God, which taketh away the sin of the world." Listening to him, John, the son of Zebedee, and Andrew, followed the Lord. Having found him, Andrew brought his brother Simon and John brought his brother James to Jesus, and when Philip was introduced to the Lord he brought his friend Nathaniel to Him. This is the apostolic way. The apostle Paul said to the Jew, "I became as a Jew, that I might gain the Jews; to them that are under the law, as under the law that I might gain them that are under the law; to them that are without law, as without law . . . that I might gain them that are without law . . . I am made all things to all men, that I might by all means save some" (1 Cor. 9:20-22). This is the spirit and the attitude all of us ought to have who name the name of our Lord.

The Need for Humility

Sometimes we are inclined to gather our righteous robes around us and to say to those on the outside, "You sinner, do not touch me, for I am in a class all by myself. You do not know all of the wonderful things that I know. Stay where you are and I will save you." I do not deny that even God puts a great difference between the Egyptians and the Israelites, between the saved and the unsaved, between the lost and those who belong to God. But at the same time I also know that when the Lord looked upon that difference He wept. Seeing the city of Jerusalem He burst into tears and said, "Jerusalem, Jerusalem, thou that killest the prophets and stonest them which are sent unto thee, how often would I have gathered thy children together, even as a hen gathereth her chickens under her wings, and ye would not" (Matt. 23:37). Jesus' feeling was a feeling of sadness and weeping and lamentation. This should be our attitude toward the world. It should never be one of superiority or condemnation — "you lost and damned sinner." We are what we are by the grace of God, that is all. I was a lost sinner but the Lord had mercy upon me and I pray that God shall have mercy on you. No greater thing does one do than to bring someone to Jesus.

Joy in Heaven

What rings the bells of glory? Luke 15 says that there is more rejoicing in the presence of the angels of God over one sinner who turns than over a multitude of people who think they need no turning. What makes heaven sing? What makes the corridors of glory ring? It is when someone comes down the aisle and says to the pastor, "Today I give my heart to Christ; I take the Lord as my Savior."

Not only is it the greatest tragedy that a soul die and be buried under a multitude of sins, and not only is it the greatest happiness when a sinner turns to the Lord. But there is a third great fact. Who is this one who is so signally blessed? Look at the text. "Brethren, if any of you do err from the truth and one convert him; let him know, that he which converteth the sinner from the error of his way, shall save a soul from death." Did you notice the emphasis? It is singular, never plural. Every pronoun and every reference of every substantive in the text is singular. Every time it is "if any" and "if one" convert him, let him know and so on. Who is that person so blessed? Does it say if a minister convert him or if an eloquent man convert him or if a great theologian convert him or if a glorious ecclesiastic convert him? No, it says "one." Now to whom does that one address his soul-saving efforts? It is still one to one. The singular is still there. I suppose many of us have wished we had the eloquence of a John Chrysostom, or could preach like George Whitefield, or were a great soul winner like Dwight L. Moody or like Billy Sunday or like Billy Graham — if we could just sway the thousands as to how glorious it would be. I do not deny it would be glorious. I would to God we all had the power to win souls as those marvelous preachers, but the text does not refer to that. It refers to one, just any one — you. It is just one saved sinner winning a lost sinner. And he who does this shall save a soul from death and shall hide a multitude of sins.

Atonement

Let us look closely at the phrase, "shall hide a multitude of sins." As I looked at it, it came to my heart that that refers to two different things. First, it refers to someone who is saved. He has been steeped in sin and when he is saved God clothes him with a robe of righteousness and hides the multitude of sins. They are covered. The word cover is translated sometimes as "atonement." When a sinner is saved, God gives him a robe of righteousness and hides his sins.

Some years ago I was shut up in prison in Alcatraz, a little island in the San Francisco bay, with one of the most noted convicts in American history. And there he gave his heart to the Lord. He told me if he ever lived beyond those prison walls, the first thing he was going to do was to come down the aisle of my church and confess his faith, and he wanted me to baptize him. After the passing of many years he was released from prison and he came down that aisle and confessed his faith in the Lord. I baptized him and he has been rejoicing ever since and testifying all over this land to the grace of God. He was a vile sinner, but now is covered with God's robe of righteousness, which hides a multitude of sins. When the prodigal came home to the father, the first thing the father did was to bring a new robe and put on him. He covered his old rags and the marks of the pig pen. Our text refers to that. Let a man know that when he converts the sinner, he saves his soul from death and hides a multitude of sins.

The phrase means something else, too, I think. It refers to the burial of all sins. They never will rise again. They never reenter the man's life. My brother, it is wonderful to save the prodigal — it is a thousand times more wonderful to keep him from being a prodigal. It is a marvelous thing to win a thief to Christ — it is a better thing to keep him from being a thief. And if you can win the child, there may be a multitude of sins that are covered over. They never appear in the child's life. How much better it is for one to give his life to Jesus in the days of his youth so he need never taste the bitterness and the dregs of violating the word and commandment of the Lord. I think that is what the phrase of our text means. If we are able to save a child not only do we save his soul from death, but we also hide a multitude of sins. The message of the Bible is that the best time to give your life to God is now. Not some other day, some other year, some other tomorrow, but now, while we have this day, this life. This is God's time. Behold, now is the day of salvation, now is the day of the Lord.